TABLE OF CON

Section	
Forward: Tips From The Top	
Message From the Author	
Why This Book Was Written	13
Getting Started Right	16
Recipe For Success...Don't Change It!	18
Basics, Basics, Basics!!!	21
Drink, Drink, Drink!!!	24
Share, Share, Share!!!	32
Listening - The Hardest Part of Sales	35
Learning the "Lingo"	39
Enagic® Ionizers	47
SD501 Features & Waters	52
The "Competition"	60
Get Trained & Independent ASAP!	84
Goal Setting	87
Effectively Sampling Kangen Water®	97
The Marketplace – You Are an Innovator!	105
Targeted Markets	111
The Medical Industry – Thrive or Alive?	138
The Beverage Industry – "Zombie Water"	147
Building Value – Eliminate the Issue of Cost	153
The 60 Second Internet Expert	155
Choosing the Right Product for Your Customer	161
The Perfect Storm	163
Play It Straight	167
Setting the Foundation	170
The Blind Leading the Blind	173
Developing Your Team	178
A Vested Interest In Your Own Success	182
Becoming a Leader	184
Attending Events: Making the Most of Them	187
Conducting Your Own Events	200
The Payment Process – Take It Step-By-Step	216
Taking Yourself Out of the Purchase Equation	223
Distributor Essentials	224
The Alkaline Water Bandwagon	243
The Future of This Project	248
So What's Next???	255

Knowledge...

*"The way of success
is the way of continuous pursuit of knowledge."*

Napoleon Hill

"The natural desire of good men is knowledge."

Leonardo da Vinci

"An investment in knowledge pays the best interest."

Benjamin Franklin

"Risk comes from not knowing what you're doing."

Warren Buffett

NOTES:

Forward: Tips From The Top

Success in this business comes with hard work, dedication and, every now and then, a little bit of good luck! But it can also come as a result of others helping you along the way.

Now, while I highly recommend that new distributors become independent as quickly as possible, I also recommend that if you find someone that is willing to help you, and if that help benefits you and your business, to take advantage of the help for as long as possible. Just don't become reliant on it!

I have been very fortunate to be able to work directly with some of the top leaders and most successful distributors in the Enagic® business and they have definitely helped me throughout my Enagic® career.

I realize that not everyone works with these people, or are even able to sit down with these individuals, so I decided to ask a few of the most successful distributors in this business for their thoughts on how a new distributor can achieve success in this project

I believe that their feedback and advice is something that every new distributor should take, which is why this section has been included in this edition of Ride The Wave.

I asked a couple of powerhouses in this business, Eli Dafesh and Robert Gridelli, to provide their best advice to help a new distributor in this business, as well as what specific steps they would take if they were brand new distributors; this is what they said...

NOTES:

Eli Dafesh

When I was asked to make a contribution to this section of the book, I really had to give it some thought. I have learned so many valuable lessons during my time in this business, and I would love to be able to share all of them with you, however I know that this section is for just a few of the most important suggestions that I feel will have the most impact and lead to the greatest chance for success in Enagic®. So, after much consideration here is my best piece of advice. In my opinion, one of the most important things for any distributor to understand is the true nature of our business. When it comes down to it we are not in the water ionizer business, the sales business or even the health and wellness business; we are in the connection business. Our business is making connections with others, cultivating those connections and teaching how to do the same thing.

To be successful in this business you have to learn how to turn a stranger into an acquaintance; then how to turn that new acquaintance into a friend; then how to turn that friend into a business partner. No matter how good your product is, if you cannot create a connection and develop a relationship with someone, your chances for success in this business will not be very good.

One of my most effective strategies is to ALWAYS look for the best in a person. Whenever I meet a new person, I find something positive about them and pay them a compliment. I follow up by asking a question like; do you keep your business options open? I also use this initial meeting as an opportunity to get a business card or contact information. Do not make the mistake of thinking that if you give someone your business card

NOTES:

that they will be calling you tomorrow to find out more. You need to proactively build your contact database by collecting contact information. This will allow you to follow up and keep in touch with new friends and potential business partners.

Building these connections actually falls right in line with the core principles of Enagic®, because one of the most important aspects of relationship building is compassion, and the idea of compassion is what Enagic® was built on. Compassion is simply caring about other people. It is remarkable how something as basic as caring for others can have such a tremendous impact. Remember, in this business our goal is not to sell, but to build relationships and share a few basic concepts with our new found friends and business partners. We share information, we share experiences, we share our water, we share good health, we share opportunity and, ultimately, we share a way to have a better life.

In addition to providing my best piece of advice, I was also asked to discuss what actions I would take if I were a new distributor. But before I cover what I would do as a new distributor, I would like to address a few points that I think are very important. I believe that we are in the relationship business, but this does not only apply to our existing and future friends. It also applies to our closest relationships with our significant others. If you are single, then this might not apply, but if you are dating or married, then pay attention.

If you have a significant other and want to be successful in this business, you really need their support. While they do not necessarily have to be an active participant in your day to day business operations, they do need to at least support what you are doing. My beautiful wife

NOTES:

Jillina has been behind me every step of the way in this business and her being supportive of my efforts has made it much easier for me to do what needs to be done. Having her support has also given me a partner in this business.

It helps to be accountable to someone other than yourself, especially towards the beginning of starting your business. We have been in the direct sales industry for a long time, so it was a lot easier for us to get focused and stay on task. Many people, however, do not have this experience, so having someone to be accountable to can help. For this, and many other reasons, it is important to have the support of your spouse or significant other.

Now, if I were a brand-new distributor one of the first things I would do is make sure I was willing to be successful in this business. I would have to ask myself some very tough questions; questions that I think every distributor should ask themselves before getting started. Am I really willing to do what it takes to be successful? Am I willing to work seven days a week to secure and build my business? Am I willing to talk to 50 people a day if that's what I have to do? When I first started in this business I asked myself these questions and I replied with a solid "YES!" to every one of them.

I believe that asking these questions is an important part of the success process. Most people are not willing to do what it takes to be successful, so before you get started, ask yourself these questions and make sure that you are not like most people. Once you have answered these questions with a yes, then it is time to really get started.

NOTES:

Now that I have answered the questions that let me know I am ready for success, I need to get focused and I can't allow anyone to steal my dreams or distract me. To help me learn what I should be doing, I will seek out others in the business that has attained the level of success that I desire, and I will shadow them. This simply means that I will watch them, learn from them and use their example to mold my own efforts.

At the same time I would be creating my calendar of events. These would be any of the product demonstrations, conference calls, trainings, luncheons or any other event or activity that could provide an opportunity for me to learn or to share information about our product or business. Once I had created my calendar, I would start calling the contacts on my list and invite them to the different events I would be attending.

In addition to using the events as opportunities to share information with my prospects I would also engage in three-way calls, using a more experienced, knowledgeable distributor to help me when talking to my prospects. I am a firm believer in the power of the three-way call. I believe that every distributor should take advantage of third-party verification that is achieved through a three-way call.

In my opinion learning how to conduct an effective three-way call is a vital part of success in this business and something that every distributor should learn to do. You should try to find two or three different people that you can call as your "expert" or "authority". Making sure that you have more than one person you can call on helps ensure that you always have someone to help with three-way call. Following up after creating interest

NOTES: _____

_____

and curiosity is just as important as the initial three-way call, so be sure you follow up every time.

As a new distributor I would also plan on hosting my own home demo in my first week. I would work hard to learn how to do a good demo and then I would do as many as possible. When I first started I did demos almost every day and I took my machine with me everywhere I went. If you are serious about success, this is the level of dedication and commitment that you need to put forth.

Jillina and I have consistently held a demo every week since we started with Enagic® and we still do. We have consistently done our Saturday morning training call since the beginning and, working together, we have never missed an event. Being consistent is extremely important. Consistency creates a habit and once something is habitual, it becomes very easy to do. I make sure I am consistent in what I do every day.

As a new distributor another thing that I would do is spend time working on myself and continue to do so every day. I would seek out books, tapes/CD's, DVD's and attend seminars and trainings. I would look for opportunities for improvement of both myself and my business, something I think every distributor should do on an ongoing basis. One of the things that I have learned along the way in my career in the direct ales industry that would really help me as a new distributor is that I don't have to be bothered by a "No". I have learned not to get emotionally attached to a "no". And it is true, that every "no" puts you closer to a "yes"!

But the reality, at least in this business, is that most of the time the "no's" are more like "not now's". Even after years of saying they we're not interested in

NOTES:

purchasing a machine, I have had contacts of mine change their minds and buy one. If you eventually want to get that "yes", just remember to share and follow up, even if it means doing it for several years. Having the right person join your business can definitely be worth the wait!

I have so much more I could share, but I will end here. I hope my advice and suggestions help you as you begin your journey as an Enagic® Distributor. I truly believe that these things can really help you succeed in this business. Remember, this is a real business and it takes time to develop a real business. You have to have patience and realize this is a 2 to 5 year project and that success can be yours, it just won't happen overnight! I wish you the best and hope for your continued success!

 Robert Gridelli

Providing a contribution to this book seemed easy enough, but then I started thinking about it; then over thinking so much that I was making things way too complicated. Then I went back to basics. Many times, as we gain experience, we tend to complicate things because we have the knowledge to do so. It might not be what we intended, but it's what we end up doing. So, with the "basics" as my guide, here is my best piece of advice to you. If you want to be successful in this business you need to take it seriously. You need to decide that this is what you're going to do. You can't allow yourself to make excuses. You have to be willing to be focused and determined to succeed.

NOTES:

What this really means is you have to become accountable to yourself. Most people in this country have never had to do this before in a business environment, but if you want to be successful, I believe this is something you have to do. Unfortunately, a lot of people say that they want to be successful, but they never take the actions or develop the mindset to make it happen. While it may seem cliché, if you want to be successful you really do have to want it. And you have to be willing to take daily action in order to get it.

When I really started working this business, I committed to becoming successful. I shared as much information and water with as many people as I could. I would take extra gallons of water with me when I left in the morning with the intention of finding someone that I could give them to throughout the course of my day. I made a commitment to not come home without giving away those extra gallons in my car. And I very, very rarely came home with any bottles of water. If you're serious about success in this business, then my advice is to take this seriously and treat this like a business. Work like this is a business, learn like this is a business, think like this is the business and what you will wind up with is a business!

Now, as far as what I would do as a new distributor; that is very easy. I would do the exact same thing I did when I was a new distributor. During my first 90 days as a distributor I became the "King" of the "Press Play Demo". Since I was still learning how to do a live demonstration, what I would do is schedule a demonstration with one of my prospects, I would bring my machine to their house, I would set it up, I would put a demonstration DVD in and while the people watched it, I filled up bottles. This is what I did for the first few months in this business. And it was very effective! You

NOTES:

can't let your lack of knowledge or experience be an excuse for you not to succeed. Since I did not know how to do the demo, I let the DVD do it for me. If I were a brand-new distributor that just started today, I would do the exact same thing. I would spend the next 90 days becoming the king of the press play demo. The only difference between then and now is there are many more resources and DVDs at our disposal, which makes this process even easier for today's distributors.

I hope this advice helps you in your career as an Enagic® Distributor. I guess my main advice is to take this business seriously and figure out how to get your business going as quickly as possible, like by doing as many press play demos as you can in your first few months. These really worked for me and I believe that these things can help you succeed in this business as well. I wish you the best!

A Sincere "Thank You" From Gerald Kostecka

I want to thank these two dynamic leaders, I greatly appreciate their contributions to this edition of RTW and I hope that you heed their suggestions and take immediate action. If you consider the incredible success these individuals have had in this business, this section contains millions of dollars' worth of wisdom, knowledge and experience. If you do not have the opportunity to meet or learn from these amazing individuals personally, then please read this section a few times and let their words resonate with you. Take advantage of these pearls of wisdom and let their advice help you secure a solid foundation on which to build your own success!

NOTES:

Message From the Author

Being introduced to Enagic® and Kangen Water® has been an absolute life changing experience for me and my family. Our overall health has greatly improved; our financial health has greatly improved; and even our mental health has greatly improved! It's funny how these three things can influence each other so profoundly.

In this Sixth Edition I have once again added a few new sections, based on input and requests from thousands of distributors. They let me know what additional information would be most helpful to them and their team members. It is my sincerest hope that the information in this book helps you as you develop your own Enagic® independent distributorship. That some of the things I have learned while building my business may help inspire the same kind of positive changes my family and I have experienced.

It is my hope that your journey is exciting & rewarding and that you meet and far exceed all of your personal goals and ambitions. You have an incredible opportunity in front of you and I hope you make the most of it!!

I truly wish you good health and great success!

NOTES:

Why This Book Was Written

I was introduced to Kangen Water® and the Enagic® Independent Distributorship program by Daniel Dimacale. He is very successful in the Enagic® business, becoming the #1 producing Independent Distributor in the world in just over one year. I've learned a lot during my time as a distributor and will be sharing some of the lessons learned, building techniques that discovered along the way and short cuts to success that I've found as I moved forward.

I had worked closely with Daniel for a number of years, prior to the Enagic® project, as a department director for a marketing company. In addition to my normal daily responsibilities, my side duties included conducting intensive research of our industry, reviewing the advancing technology, checking out our competition and staying in front of the latest hi-tech methods of marketing and communication.

It also included development of marketing campaigns, marketing materials and online / Internet resources. In short, I had to become an expert in nearly every aspect of our business and industry in order to effectively do my job, which is exactly what I did.

When I officially connected to the Enagic® program Daniel asked me to "get up to speed" on *this* product and *this* industry, so I rolled up my sleeves and got to work. I immersed myself in everything I could find about ionizers. I started reading as many books as I could find. I spent countless hours online, digging as deeply as I could, to learn about the history of the technology, the science behind it, the roots of the company, the different manufacturers, the claims, the myths, the facts, the benefits, the drawbacks; basically

NOTES:

everything. Just like before, I needed to research and study as much as I could in order to be effective with *this* product and business, which is exactly what I did.

Within a few months I was up to speed and had a pretty well rounded knowledge and understanding of ionizers and the newly developing U.S. marketplace. I helped Daniel by answering technical questions and filling in the gaps of his understanding of ionization and he helped me by providing support and guidance in the ways of successfully building a business in this project.

As our businesses grew Daniel started referring other team members to me with their questions and I quickly became the team "answer guy". This newly designated distinction quickly spread throughout the entire Kangen1 Organization and eventually to distributors that were in no way connected to either Daniel or me. It was at this point that my phone started ringing constantly. Every day someone was calling, wanting to know something. I soon discovered that many of the questions being asked were the same. I found myself telling different people the same basic information numerous times throughout the course of a day.

Now don't get me wrong, I was happy to help out, no matter who it was or what team they were on, it's just that I was getting so many calls every day from people outside of my business that it started to affect the time I had available to provide support and to answer the questions of my own team members. That was the motivation for writing this book. I wanted to give anyone with the desire to excel in this business access to the information that I believe can help them be successful, whether I was available or not.

NOTES:

So, I filled these pages with how I answer the questions that I am asked most, in straight forward, easy to understand explanations. I wrote this as simply as I could, in laymen's terms, with many examples and situations, covering the most frequently asked questions, the most wondered about strategies and the most confusing aspects of how to be effective in this business.

In my opinion, everything you really need to know to get started on the road to becoming a successful Independent Enagic® Distributor is in your hands right now. So remember, if you are not sure of something, you don't need to call me...just read this book!

Are you excited to start your journey? Then say it with me...

I'M READY...

I'M SET...

HERE I GO!!

NOTES:

Getting Started Right

We're going to jump right into this book with me sharing the secret to success as an Enagic® Independent Distributor. The secret is that there is no secret!! While there is no secret, there is, however, a process. In fact, there is a process for just about everything we do as a distributor. Almost every aspect of this business can be broken down into simple, step-by-step processes. Learning and putting these processes into action will definitely help you on your way to success.

While it is true that there is no secret formula to success in this project, there are techniques and strategies that, when combined with simple step-by-step processes, can definitely bring success more swiftly.

Much of this book is dedicated to explaining the most important of these processes and some of the most effective techniques and strategies. We will go into the when's, the how's and the why's of each. My goal is to empower you with what I have learned over the last few years and to allow you to quickly and efficiently learn what you will really need to succeed.

NOTES:

One of the keys to getting started right is having the right attitude. While it is probably a bit cliché, it is true that attitude is everything! Good or bad, your attitude greatly influences all aspects of your life. In order to get the most out of this book, be sure that your attitude is properly aligned and prepared to make the most of it!

You are embarking on what could be the most incredible journey of your lifetime. While you are most likely filled with enthusiasm and excitement, you also need to be willing to learn, be open minded to new ideas and be determined to succeed. Along with all of this you need to have an above average, absolutely unbelievably positive attitude. With these things, you will be unstoppable!

I truly believe that having a positive attitude, coupled with the correct knowledge, can be the difference between a rough ride and an amazing journey in this project. The attitude is ultimately up to you, all I can do is provide you with the correct knowledge; information, tips and suggestions that worked for me and many other people in this project.

So please, get started right and take this book seriously. Take notes and highlight sections that are of greatest importance to you. Treat this book like it can change your financial future, because, if used correctly, it can!

NOTES:

Recipe For Success...Don't Change It!

One of the keys to success in this business is being able to master what someone else has already figured out how to do! Sounds easy enough, right? You would think so, but the reality is that most people are not satisfied with simply copying what another person has perfected. They are convinced that they can come up with a better way to do things. Build a better mousetrap, so to speak.

NOTES:

Let me be very clear about the following point: those who truly succeed in this industry and this project are imitators, not innovators!!

A very effective formula for success in this business has already been developed; all you have to do is learn it and then master it. It's like a recipe for a delicious gourmet meal that you would find in a cookbook.

When you buy a cookbook, you do so because the person that put it together is able to cook better than you, which is why you want to follow their directions. They have spent the time and energy figuring out just the right amounts, flavors and ingredients to create the final epicurean delight.

I'm sure you can imagine what would happen if the ingredients, amounts and directions of a recipe were changed. They would probably wind up making a big, disgusting mess that tastes horrible. Why do some people feel compelled to change things and risk creating a master flop instead of a masterpiece? Why would they not follow the recipe that they know works? Why do they chance messing everything up?

Well, this project is just like a cookbook. The recipe already exists. You should concentrate on learning how to follow the recipe to the letter and how to make the dish perfectly, every time.

Don't let temptation get the best of you and start trying new things. Learn how to do what works and what has created the most success. Some people feel that duplicating a process created by someone else somehow makes them less of who they are. This is completely incorrect!

NOTES:
_____

Duplicating a process does not mean you can't be yourself. Once you learn how to do things, your personality and personal style will shine through. It's learning the process in the first place that is important. The easiest way to learn it is to simply copy what is working for the most successful people. Imitation may be the sincerest form of flattery, but in this business it is also the quickest way to success!!

So learn the recipe, follow the recipe and teach your new distributors the recipe and cook up a huge helping of success!!!

NOTES:

Basics, Basics, Basics!!!

If you are going to follow my advice, and the advice of the top producing distributors, then the first things you need to do are to learn and to master the basics of the project. This project is not complicated; however it is also not easy. While it is true that what you really need to learn in order to be successful is fairly simple, you are still going to have to work to be successful. How smart and how hard you are willing to work will determine just how successful you will become.

I say "how smart" because working smart is just as important as working hard, maybe more so. In this project working smart means following the formula and using the most successful people in the project as your example of what to do. Remember, don't change the recipe!! If you mix this, with hard work and determination, then success should be easily attained.

So, now all you really need to do is learn and master the basics. In this project we really only do three things: Share the Product (give away water), Share the Opportunity (let people know about the business) and Promote Events (invite prospects / distributors to upcoming events / presentations / trainings). Knowing how to do these three things can be the most important skills you can have in this project.

Now let's discuss how to master these skills. The first, and usually the easiest, is through repetition... doing these things over and over and over. Just like any skill, you will hone and refine these skills with practice. You will get better at each piece as you do them more. You will be better at sharing the product the tenth time then you were the second. Why? Because along the way you are learning more about the product, you are

NOTES:

hearing stories about the water, you are personally experiencing how the water can help. All of these things end up making you more effective at what you are doing. You have to realize that you are not supposed to be perfect at this when you start! None of us were!

In the beginning you are going to say the wrong thing, do the wrong thing and mess things up. That's part of the learning process. Screwing up in the beginning is what helps you fine tune what you say, how you say it, when you say it and even creates a better understanding of why you say it.

It is also very important to allow your referring distributor or a more experienced distributor who you are working with to help guide you as you are starting. Arrange to accompany them on a few water sample deliveries. Tag along with them to some presentations and trainings. Listen to what they say. How they invite people to events. What they tell new prospects about the water. Their experience can be an excellent free resource for you, but only if you take advantage of it!

As you are beginning, you want to learn as much as possible, from as many people as possible, hopefully successful people. I do not suggest that you connect yourself with someone that is not successful because you will learn bad habits that will be difficult to break later down the road. And if your referring distributor is new to the program, then both of you should connect with a more experienced, successful distributor and both of you should start learning together.

Keep in mind that it is always better to connect with someone that is within your referral line, meaning that they have some degree of financial interest in your success. In many cases what starts as a financial

NOTES:

interest becomes a personal interest, which, in this business, is an awesome combination. The financial connection will initially help motivate them to help you and support your business growth.

In some cases a distributor from a different line, meaning that your production has zero financial impact on them, may be willing to work with you and help you out. This only happens if a distributor takes a personal interest in you. It is important to remember that these people have no obligation to work with you, nor should you have any expectations that they will do so. Most distributors are more than willing to help out, just be sure not to push too hard or ask for too much. This is a sure fire way to get them to not want to help you.

Since I am talking about getting assistance, let me address an important point that I want to make very clear to every person reading this book. Many people believe that because a person is "referred" by someone else into this business that their referrer has some sort of obligation to help them. While it is true that the vast majority do help, the reality is that your success rests in the hands of one person and one person only...YOU!!

The best approach for success in this business and this industry is to NEVER worry about or expect anything from those "above" you. If help comes from those above you, great, but if it does not, it should not affect your chances at success at all! If you decide right here and now to make your success your own responsibility, then your chances of making it happen are vastly improved. However, if you decide that your success is going to be contingent on someone else's efforts and support, you might as well prepare for disappointment and failure.

NOTES:

Seriously commit to your own success by making the decision to succeed. Don't allow the support, or lack thereof, of someone else to become your excuse to succeed or fail. Develop this mindset and teach it to your people. You will end up creating a sales organization that is independent and self-sufficient, which should be one of your ultimate goals.

Now I don't want you to think that you are going to end up being all alone and working this project all by yourself. Most serious distributors work very hard to help their referred distributors. My point is to not let that help be the deciding factor to your success.

That said, what you will want to do is commit to learning and mastering the basics, in whatever way necessary. With the help of your referring distributor, a mentoring distributor or on your own, whichever works for you is what you should do. The important piece is that you recognize the importance of basics; that know and understand them and that you practice them on a daily basis!

Drink, Drink, Drink!!!

Most new distributors do not realize just how important drinking Kangen Water® is to their success in this project. Let me tell you, it is probably one of the most important things you can do! You have to realize that the water is the glue that sticks most people to this product and business. It is the way the water works for them. It is the benefits they receive from drinking the water and the benefits they see friends and loved ones experiencing.

Hearing the countless stories of the benefits the water has had for people is one thing, but personally

NOTES: _____

experiencing them is something altogether different. It takes your personal belief in the product to an entirely new level. It can make you impervious to any skepticism, negative comments or challenges to the validity of what you are doing. It can make you bullet proof...once you are there, you might as well get a cape and a shirt with a big "S" on it!!!

But the only way to get to that point is to drink, drink, drink!! Make sure you take drinking the water seriously. Make it a priority for yourself. Drink it at home, take a bottle with you to work, even take it to restaurants when you go out to eat. Heck this can actually be a door opener for a potential prospect. I don't want to get too far off the topic, but let me quickly explain what I mean.

When my family goes out to eat we all take our bottles, filled with Kangen Water®, with us. When we sit down one of the first things the waiter or waitress asks us is if we would like something to drink. This question is actually a door opener for me, but like everything there is a process, even in my response. Here are the actual steps I take...

First, I respond to their inquiry with a statement that will most likely spark their interest, "Actually, we are probably going to have the most unique drink order of the night..." The reaction is almost always the same, a questioning look, followed by "try me". I then reply with "we are going to need three empty glasses, no ice, with three straws."

They actually initiate the second step with their reaction. The look they have at this point is almost always the same, a bit puzzled. They are obviously trying to process this request, to make sense of it, which they can't do because they do not have a reference point to

NOTES:

draw from, this is a never before heard request. I then offer up a little more information, which allows them to understand the request, "we drink a special water" and then I hold up my bottle. They will typically nod a few times and say "Okay..." and they are off to grab the empty glasses.

When they bring the glasses to the table, they usually, once again, initiate the final step in this process. They will almost always say, "so, what is so special about that water?" Every time I am asked this question it is like a door opening and they are inviting me to come on in! I will then tell them a little about the water and I make sure to speak loud enough to be overheard by the surrounding tables, you never know who might be listening! Of course, you should never be obnoxiously loud or anything, just enough to be heard above the chatter of the restaurant. I have actually ended up sampling several restaurant employees, and even one couple from a neighboring table, by using this approach.

The point of explaining this to you was not to teach you a new prospecting technique, even though that is exactly what I just did; it is to emphasize the importance of making the water a part of your daily routine.

It is also very important that you commit to drinking the water because you will be setting an example for those around you. When others see that you are serious about drinking the water, they tend to take it more seriously. You have to realize the mixed message you would be sending if you are telling people about the benefits of the water, but every time they actually see you, you have a Starbucks coffee or fast food large drink cup with you. Having your water bottle with you shows them that you take drinking this water seriously!

NOTES:
_____

The most important reason to drink the water is to develop your own personal testimonial. Nothing is more convincing then telling someone your own experience. There is an old sales saying, "Facts tell, stories sell", meaning that facts provide people with information; while stories inform them of practical application of the information and how it might pertain to them. Until you have your own personal experience all you are doing is relaying facts about the water. Once you have your own story, telling people about the water drastically changes.

I found this to be very true in my own experience with the water. You see, when I first started working on this project, I did so by doing research, but refusing to actually drink the water. I was being stubborn and very closed minded. Looking back, I guess I was one of the biggest skeptics I had ever met!

The research I was doing kept pointing to pretty incredible things, but my lack of personal experience was keeping me from really caring about what the water might do for me and my family. After several months of doing research and compiling information, and my wife requesting that we try the water, I finally agreed to give the water a chance.

It is funny how sometimes the biggest "personal" impact can actually come from something that happens to someone else, which is exactly what happened in my case. This is also a very important lesson, which I will address in a few moments. But let me tell you what happened. The second day into our sampling of the water my son, 12 years old at the time, came to me with a look of concern.

NOTES:

"Dad, I need to talk to you." There was a sense of urgency in his voice which immediately grabbed my attention. I told him to shut the door and sit down.

"What's going on?" I asked.

"Well, I think there may be something wrong with me." He paused for a moment, and then continued, "my pee smells really bad."

I was a bit perplexed and responded by simply asking, "What??"

He continued, "My pee smells really bad. I think there may be something really wrong with me, it's freakin' me out."

In order to better understand the situation I asked him to describe the way it smelled.

"Remember when we went to Las Vegas for your birthday and we ate at the Eiffel Tower Restaurant and had that really good asparagus soup?" he asked, "remember what happened when we got back to the condo? Well, it smells worse than that!"

I did remember and it gave me a good understanding of what he was experiencing. For those of you that do not know, there is a digestive enzyme that produces methyl mercaptan when it breaks down asparagus. This is the same chemical which gives a skunk its defensive smell. The asparagus breaks down quickly in the body and the enzyme releases the methyl mercaptan, which eventually goes through the kidneys and is excreted as a waste product in the urine, which can then have a very pungent odor. I thought about it and realized that he was experiencing the detox effect of the water. That his

NOTES:

body was expelling toxins and that they were coming out in his urine. I started to explain this to him but he stopped me about half way through my explanation.

"Yeah, but Dad, that's not all. It's green."

"What's green?" I asked.

"My pee. It's green." He replied.

"You mean its greenish?"

"Nope, it's green like Kermit the Frog green! It's really green!"

"Well, how do you feel?"

"I feel fine, it's just really weird."

I went on to finish my explanation of the detox effect and told him to keep an eye on it for the next couple of days and to let me know if it continued. About 5 or 6 hours later that same day I was working on my computer in my home office and my wife came in and shut the door.

"Honey, I need to talk to you."

"Yeah, what's up?" I asked, paying more attention to my work on the computer than to my wife's request to talk.

"Hey, stop what you're doing; I really need to talk to you."

"I'm listening" I replied as I continued to type and not really listen.

NOTES: _____

My wife gave me a little whack in the arm and said, "I'm serious, I need to talk to you!"

The whack got my attention, as this is not something she would normally do. I stopped what I was doing and turned to her.

"Honey, I think there might be something wrong with me, my pee smells really bad."

I kind of chuckled at her statement and replied "And it's green, right?"

"How did you know that??" she replied, with a puzzled look on her face.

"Well sweetheart, our son, whom you home school and spend almost all your time with, came to me a few hours ago with the exact same thing. I told him that he must be detoxing from drinking the water and I guess that you are too."

The next day both of them were fine, no more odor or color. But that experience really got my attention. It made me take the water much more seriously. My own direct personal experience would not come for several more months, when we stopped sampling and we bought our own machine. It was then that I saw results first hand. In the first two months of owning our machine my overall health improved, I was feeling better and I had a lot more energy which, needless to say, thoroughly convinced me the Kangen Water® really was different.

I mentioned earlier that what happened with my wife and son was actually an important lesson. The lesson is that the experience that gets the attention of a person

NOTES:

might not always be their own. Sometimes it is the experience of a parent, a sibling, a best friend or a child. For me, it was the experience of my wife and son that woke me up and made me pay closer attention. This is one of the reasons that you want to be sure to offer water for friends and family members of everyone you are sampling! They might end up with the same type of situation and may end up compelled to purchase a machine based on what the water has done for someone they care about!

When it comes to drinking the water, just remember that the water is the bridge that connects everything in this project. It is important for you to drink the water and to cross the bridge from skeptic to believer. The only way you can do that is to drink the water and experience the benefits first hand!

NOTES:

Share, Share, Share!!!

I have already explained the importance of drinking the water in the last section and now it is time for you to take the next step, which is to share the water with other people. In the development of your business, this is one of the most important things you can and will do! As such, it is vital that you become proficient in giving away free water!

So, when it comes to sharing the water, where should you start? Let me begin by discussing where you should NOT start. Many times a new distributor joins the business and is full of ideas of how they will explode. They think that they have tons of new ideas and that they will set new sales records. They are sure that THEY will be the one to capture some specific market or industry.

If you are "THEY", then please allow me to bring you back to reality. First, no matter what your brilliant idea or strategy, someone who has come before you has thought of it or tried it; and it did not work! Come to grips with this fact now and you will save yourself a lot of time and effort! How do I know it did not work? Because if it did, it is what everyone would be doing.

Since it is not, it obviously did not work and you should not waste your time! Sure, everyone would like to find a way to sell 100 machines to a big company. We would all like to figure out the way to get a machine in every health food store across the nation. We would like to be the one to sell a machine to the biggest fitness center in the country. Of course we would!! But people have already tried and it has not worked. Not because it can't, but because the introduction of the technology to this marketplace is not to that point yet.

NOTES:

You have to understand that approaching a large corporation is a time consuming process and one that is filled with red tape and formality. Unless you are the CEO, it is going to take a long time, if it ever happens at all, for you to have success!

Trying to land that HUGE account is a practice I call "Whale Hunting". Instead of trying to land a whale with one throw of the harpoon, learn how to catch a small fish with a pole. Then keep practicing until you become skilled at catching a single fish. This is something that once you master, you can teach others, which is the key to BIG success in this project!

The funny thing about whale hunting is that all the time a person is wasting looking for a whale, there are TONS of small fish swimming all around them. Enough small fish to feed a person for a lifetime, but they become so fixated on landing that whale that they ignore all those small fish and then end up starving to death!! Don't let this happen to you!!

Become a master at fishing for the individual fish and you will do just fine! This is where sharing the water comes into play, because the water is the best "bait" we have found!! It is what secures a prospect to the hook and allows you to reel them in for the sale. The funny thing is that, if you learn how to share the water correctly, you won't even have to reel your fish in, they will jump right into your boat all by themselves!

I will be discussing some of the different strategies of sampling water in later sections, but for right now, you just need to give water to everyone that will drink it! So, who are the best people to start with?

NOTES:

Well, the best people to share the water with are known by a variety of different names: "warm market", "circle of influence", "mom", "dad", "brother", "sister", etc. Basically they are the people in your life that meet two criteria. First, they are people that you genuinely care about and would like to see their health improve. Second, they will listen to you, just because you are you. This means that they will try the water just because you are the person asking them to.

This is very important when you first start in this business, because you WILL mess up!! You will say the wrong thing; you will do the wrong thing; you will basically screw up! Since you're going to screw up, it is much better to screw up with people that will be forgiving! That will not discount the potential of the water just because you did not explain it correctly. This is one of the main reasons you should start your sharing efforts with people you know.

When you're more experienced and knowledgeable then you can share the water with people that you don't know as well, or at all. But wait until you know enough about the water to be able to answer questions. Remember, when you first start you are supposed to mess up!! You are learning a lot of new things and you are excited, which can actually be a very dangerous combination!

Let your sponsor or your mentor in the business help you as you get started, they can teach you the proper ways to sample while you are learning. Focus your sharing efforts on people that you know and get the mindset that, "If someone I know gets near me, they're gonna get wet!!"

NOTES:

Listening — The Hardest Part of Sales

Many people are under the impression that being successful in sales is about providing a prospect with as much information as is humanly possible. About having a slick, well-rehearsed sales pitch that will dazzle any prospect to the point of whipping out the check book and inking the deal. In reality, nothing could be farther from the truth. Of course, there is something to be said about being able to answer questions and sounding like you know what you are talking about, but what successful sales really boils down to is listening. This is where so many new distributors really have a problem.

Let me explain what typically happens and I think you will understand how and why it becomes problematic. When you first become an Enagic® Independent Distributor you are EXCITED!!! You've probably been getting water samples and have been feeling better. You may have seen a few DVD's or maybe even a few live presentations. You finally purchased your own machine and it is quickly becoming part of your daily routine. You are being exposed to so much new information and you are soaking it up like a sponge and now you want to share it with everyone you know. So you start talking and talking and talking...

It is at this point that things go south! You are so busy telling people things that you've learned or that you find interesting that you fail to recognize what it is that they really need to know or want to find out about. It's like dumping a 55 gallon drum of Kangen Water® on someone that says their thirsty instead of just giving them a glass. I know you will be tempted to spew forth everything you know, but you need to resist. Implement the following technique: Shut Up! Zip It! Be Quiet!

NOTES:

Hush! Don't give in to the temptation to flex your mental muscles and show off how much you have learned. Instead, share only what you need to share to accomplish your goal, which we will discuss in just a minute.

The approach that I recommend is sharing the water in "shot glass" portions. Now, I don't mean this literally, I mean it figuratively, in regards to sharing information. And if you don't know what a shot glass is, it is a little tiny glass, do you get the point? You have to know your goal, what it is you are trying to accomplish when you are talking to someone about the water. All you are trying to do is get them interested enough to be willing to try the water. So give them small amounts, "shot glasses", of information in order to stimulate their curiosity. Make sure that you are not dousing them with so much water information that they feel like they are drowning!!

There is an old proverbial phrase that dates back to the late 15th century, "Too Much Of A Good Thing", meaning that excess of anything may do harm. This is definitely true in this business. If a person feels overwhelmed with what you are telling them, they will probably not be as receptive. Don't make it difficult or confusing for a person to want to try the water. Give each person just enough of what they need in order to decide to give it a try, then STOP talking. Or you could find yourself talking them out of trying the water.

Here is an example that I think just about everyone can understand. Most people enjoy chocolate. It is sweet, delicious and is even rumored to work as a mild aphrodisiac. In moderation, chocolate can be an incredible treat. But have you ever eaten too much chocolate? Remember back when you were a kid and

NOTES: _____

you over did it a bit with some sweets? To really understand my point, imagine sitting down and eating a full pound of chocolate. Having the sweetness become so overwhelming that it makes your teeth hurt. Having so much chocolate in your system that your stomach gurgles and you actually feel ill. Believe it or not, this is the exact same effect you can have on a prospect when you give them too much information.

Remember that they have not been exposed to this information over a period of time, like you were. You are trying to give them several weeks' worth of information in just a matter of minutes. I know everyone has the best of intentions, but you really have to recognize what effect you are ACTUALLY HAVING, not what effect you intended on having.

Now that you know the hazards of talking too much about the water, let's address the aspect of listening. Make sure that you are really listening to people when you talk to them about the water. They will tell you everything you'll need to know to help them make a trying or buying decision.

Remember that the reasoning behind a person deciding to try the water or eventually buys a machine is always different. Don't make the mistake of thinking that what got you to try the water or buy a machine is what will make someone else do it. And don't make the mistake of taking a "one size fits all" approach when speaking with people. Let me explain what I mean.

Every person you speak to is different and they will have different issues, different motivations and different triggers, which are the things that really capture their interest. Talking to someone about acid reflux that doesn't have acid reflux is not going to end up being

NOTES:

very productive. While it is true that providing general information can be effective, it is much better to listen to the prospect and then speak to them about what matters to THEM. Listening is the only way you will ever know what it is that they need to know! Then give them the information that they want. A good sales person is someone that has the ability to listen and then can provide information based on what they heard, it's as easy as that!

In order to be effective it is important to have a well-rounded knowledge of the water and how it has helped people, this allows you to speak to more people and address more issues. Make sure that you are always learning more; that you are seeking out information that will make your listening more productive.

I am constantly looking for new information and, even up to the time of writing of this book, I typically learn something new on a daily basis. The easiest way to expand your knowledge is to talk to more experienced distributors, listen to people when they are speaking about their personal experiences, read books written by experts, attend live meetings and get to as many training opportunities as possible!

So, what is the lesson you should take away from this section? Listening is a key component to success in this project. You should make becoming a great listener one of your priorities!

NOTES:

Learning the "Lingo"

As with just about every industry, technology and product, there are certain terms or phrases that are specific to them. It is important that you be familiar with some of the more common terms and phrases that pertain to our industry and product. It is not necessary to become an expert in the formal terminology of all things related or pertaining to ionizers to be effective. But it is important that you master the basics, including our most widely and frequently used terms. The following list is by no means the only ones you should learn, but they are probably the ones you will use the most. These definitions are in "layman's" terms, meaning they have been drastically simplified. If you want in depth definitions for these terms, seek out a really good dictionary or encyclopedia. These are quick definitions, for the purpose of building general knowledge and basic understanding.

Continuous Ionized Electrolysis Water Generator – This is the official name of the ionized water devices manufactured and sold by Enagic®. While this is the official name of the product, it is often referred to as a "water machine" or simply as a "machine". For the sake of basic, day-to-day conversations, using the word "machine" is probably the most simple and effective way to refer to the product.

Kangen Water – The term "Kangen" is Japanese, roughly translated to mean "return to origin" and "Kangen Water" is the registered trademark of Enagic®. Some people ask why Mr. Ohshiro insisted on going through the time, trouble and expense of trade marking the name of the water produced by the machine. The answer was very simple; Mr. Ohshiro is a student of business history, and he knows, based on countless

NOTES:

examples, when your product is the best in the industry, you give it an identity. Of course, Enagic® could have saved money by simply referring to the water made by their machines by its technical name, "alkaline ionized water", but in order to give the quality of the water the respect and honor it deserves, it had to be given a name which would set it apart. While the trademarked term for the water produced by the machines is "Kangen Water", the official industry term for this type of water is "alkaline ionized water". This is the term we recommend distributors use if providing a more in-depth description of Kangen Water. It should be noted that the word "Kangen" has more significance in Enagic than to just describe a type of water; this word is actually part of a bigger Enagic philosophy. In the same spirit of a "return to origin", it is the concept of stripping away the things that keep us from arriving at a state of balance and harmony. Enagic actually promotes five different types of "Kangen": *Bodily Constitution* = Good Health, *Fair & High Income* = Good Earnings, *Quick Return* = Rapid Financial Reward, *Appreciation / Compassion* = Care of Self & Others and *Societal Support* = Care of the Community.

pH – This is the acronym for Power / Potential of Hydrogen, which is represented by a scale, ranging from 0 – 14, that measures if a solution is acidic, neutral or alkaline. The pH scale measurement is based on the amount of hydrogen ion (H+) activity in a solution. A solution is acidic, which is below 7 on the pH scale, when it has more free hydrogen activity, and alkaline, which is above 7 on the pH scale, when there is a lack of free hydrogen activity. The letters of its name are derived from the absolute value of the power / potential (*p*) of the hydrogen ion concentration (*H*).

NOTES:

Alkaline – On the pH scale, anything that measures above neutral, 7.0 pH, is considered and called alkaline.

Acidic – On the pH scale, anything that measures below neutral, 7.0 pH, is considered and called acidic.

ORP – This is the acronym for Oxidation Reduction Potential, which is a measurement that determines if something is an antioxidant, which will have a negative reading, such as -300; or if something is an oxidant, which will have a positive reading, such as 300. This measurement is typically taken with an ORP Meter, which has been designed and calibrated to measure the ORP of liquids.

Plates – This refers to the metal plates that are found in the electrolysis chamber in a water ionizer. The plates are what conduct the electricity, with either a positive or negative charge, during the electrolysis process. The plates are one of the most important components of an ionizer, as they dictate the strength and longevity of the properties of ionized water. The size and amount of power surging through the plates are what create the properties, so larger plates, with greater power are preferred.

Electrolysis / Ionization – This is the process by which water is passed over negatively and positively charged plates and is physically split into two separate streams. The negatively charged water is alkaline and the positively charged water is acidic.

Electrolysis Chamber – This is essentially the "engine" of a water ionizer. It is where the source water comes in contact with the positively and negatively charged plates and is split into two separate streams of water. The actual size of the plates and the amount of

NOTES:

electricity surging through them normally dictate the size and construction of the electrolysis chamber. Obviously, a more solid construction and larger size is needed for a water ionizer with bigger plates and more power. The SD501 has one of the largest and most powerful electrolysis chambers of any water ionizer on the market. In fact, even the electrolysis chamber of the LeveLuk R, which is a basic starter unit and has the smallest plate size and lowest power output of all the Enagic® water ionizers, is larger and better constructed than most of the other brands best water ionizers.

Free Radical – These are unstable, chemically incomplete substances that 'steal' electrons from other molecules. They are highly reactive, potentially causing damage in the body to things such as cells and natural enzymes, making them less effective. Free radicals occur naturally as by-products of the body's use of oxygen and creation of energy. Once in the body, free radicals can damage tissues and delicate cell membranes. They may even accelerate the ageing process. Our bodies do have a natural defense system to deal with free radicals; however, studies are finding that the average American lifestyle is creating an overwhelming abundance of free radicals and that our natural defense system is not adequately protecting us. For this reason many people need to ingest foods and beverages containing antioxidants, which can donate electrons to the free radicals, quelling their hyper-reactivity and rendering them harmless.

Antioxidant – These are substances or nutrients in foods and beverages, having a negative oxidation reduction potential, which can prevent or slow oxidative damage to our body. Oxidation, which is a regular function of metabolism and cell function, strips an electron from certain molecules. These molecules,

NOTES:

called free radicals, must then steal an electron from a nearby molecule to repair themselves; which means that the nearby molecule must now steal an electron from another molecule and so on and so on. This vicious oxidation cycle ends when an electron is taken from a molecule which has an excess electron available to donate. Antioxidants act as "free radical scavengers" by donating the excess electron to the free radical, which quells their hyper-reactivity and renders them harmless. Many of the serious health problems facing American's today are attributed to oxidative damage. Antioxidants may also act as powerful immune defense enhancers, which may reduce the risk of disease. Alkaline water is a very effective natural antioxidant because of its very high negative oxidation reduction potential.

Flow Rate – This term describes the amount of water that flows through an ionizer. The flow rate is an important consideration if a consumer is comparing different brands of ionizers. The SD501 has a flow rate of 7 liters per minute, while the majority of other ionizer brands are between 1.5 liters and 3 liters per minute. The reason for this sizable difference is the size and power of the plates. The SD501 has 7 large plates, with 230 watts of power, which will sufficiently ionize water, even at a high flow rate. Many of the other brands have a regulator / flow restrictor built into their machines, which physically restricts the water flow in order for their smaller and less powerful plates to ionize the water. Some of the other brands promote this as a positive feature, and even a selling point. However, in reality, this is simply a necessary component for these lower quality machines to produce alkaline water at all.

Source Water – The water that flows from the faucet being used by the machine. The term is often used to

NOTES:

- 43 -

illustrate that every location has different source water and there are many factors that determine its quality.

PPM – This is a water industry term you will probably never be faced with or have to use, however you may run into someone in the water industry who tries to test your knowledge by asking the PPM of certain chemicals / minerals in Kangen Water®. The easiest response is that Kangen Water® originates as tap water before filtration or ionization, so the PPM is no higher than allowable by municipal water rules and regulations. Just in case someone ever does try this with you, here is what it actually means: PPM is the acronym which stands for Parts Per One Million. This water industry terms is used to describe the ratios which show a concentration of one substance compared to another, usually by weight. When this measurement is associated with a solution, PPM would more accurately be designated as milligrams per liter. For example, if a water sample is tested and determined to have 10 PPM of Nitrate, this solution has 10 milligrams of Nitrate per liter of water. If a water test shows 50 PPM of Lead, it would more accurately be expressed as 50 milligrams of Lead per liter of water, and so on. It is very difficult to fully understand a term such as PPM, but it can be important if you run into someone that is in the water industry. It usually helps to compare the term to common everyday measurements. For example: a part per million is like one inch in 16 miles or one drop in 35 gallons.

TDS – This is another water industry term that you will probably never be faced with or have to use, however you may run into someone in the water industry that tries to test your knowledge by asking about the TDS in Kangen Water®. Again, the easiest response is that Kangen Water® originates as tap water before filtration or ionization, so the TDS is no higher than allowable by municipal water rules and regulations. Just in case someone ever does try this with you, here is what it actually means: TDS is the acronym that stands for Total Dissolved Solids. This water industry term is used to describe solids in water that can pass through a filter and as the measurement of the amount of those solids that have been dissolved in water. These solids can include carbonate, bicarbonate, chloride, sulfate, phosphate, nitrate, calcium, magnesium, potassium, sodium, organic ions, and other ions. Certain levels of these ions in water are necessary for good health. However, TDS concentrations which are too high or too low, can lead to health issues.

pH Drops – Also known as "pH Test Liquid". This is an ethanol solution that reacts with liquids based on the pH level of the liquid. When added to clear liquids the solution reacts by changing the color of the liquid to the appropriate color that is represented by the pH color chart. The pH Test Liquid available directly from Enagic® is recommended. The colors of the different pH levels are consistent with the pH color charts provided by Enagic®. Not all testing liquids change the color of liquid the same, so be sure you have the correct color chart for the testing fluid that you are using.

Enhancer Fluid – The enhancer fluid is only used during production of the 11.5 pH & 2.5 pH waters. It is mostly purified water, like 99%+, then there is a small amount of sodium chloride, also known as table salt. The sodium chloride does two things, first the salt in the water allows the machine to utilize its power better, as the salt acts as an additional conductor for the electricity. There is also a reaction between the salt, the water and the electricity which creates a natural form of bleach; this water comes out of the bottom the gray hose. I say

NOTES:
_____

"natural", as it has germ killing abilities, but you can drink it and not need to be rushed to the hospital, like regular bleach would do.

Phenol Red - This is the technical name of the pH testing drops that are used in the product demo to show the different pH levels of clear beverages. For consistency sake, and to make sure your reaction colors correspond with the free pH chart you received with your machine, we recommend using the drops offered by Enagic®.

Tipping Point - Every person is different and every person has a different "Tipping Point". To me the tipping point is when the body goes back into a state of balance and is strong enough to effectively restart the self-healing process. Some people are unable to reach their tipping point during sampling, which is why they see little to no noticeable or visible benefit during this time. Sometimes it takes having a machine and drinking fresh water consistently to reach the tipping point.

Ironically, I was one of those people. During the 3 months that I sampled the water I saw very little personal benefit. My wife and son were seeing benefits, which is what kept my attention and my willingness to continue sampling. It was not until we purchased our SD501 and I was drinking the water consistently, at full potency, that I personally passed my tipping point.

These are probably the most widely used terms as you get started. Be sure to learn these terms and listen for other important terms and phrases along your journey as an independent distributor. It is very important to know what you are talking about when speaking with prospects. As I have said before, you don't have to be an expert, but you should at least know the basics!!

NOTES:
_____

Enagic® Ionizers

To be effective in sales you need to know your product. The LeveLuk SD501 is the #1 selling Enagic® ionizer, but there are other models available for every consumer need. Understanding each model allows you to recommend the best choice for your prospects.

There are basically two different kinds of ionizer purchases: an end-user and a distributor. If your prospect is strictly going to be an end-user, then the machine for them is the one that meets all their needs, but if the person is going to be a distributor, then they need an SD501. This machine will fulfill both their personal and professional needs, which is why this is the one they need.

The differences between machines really boil down to the way it will be used and by how many people. The following is a brief description of each machine and the type of user for which each is intended. Oh, and one more thing, it is not necessary for you to become an ionizer expert in order to effectively sell. Knowing how the different machines will meet the needs of your customer is all you really need to know.

LeveLuk R

The LeveLuk R is equipped with 3 small electrodes and produces Kangen® alkaline drinking water, clean water and beauty water. With a smaller, compact body, the LeveLuk R was designed to function as a basic, starter unit. The pH range of the R is 4.5 – 9.5. The product comes with a 3-year warranty.

NOTES:

The LeveLuk R was introduced to replace the Sun-US, which was a travel unit and was never intended to be a full-time use machine. The Sun-US was originally designed to be a secondary, portable machine.

The LeveLuk R was redesigned to be used as a basic functionality, full-use machine. While it does not offer the option of making 11.5 pH or 2.5 pH waters, it does create all 3 grades of alkaline drinking water 8.5, 9.0 & 9.5.

For a smaller machine, the properties are strong and will last throughout the day. However, the water produced by the LeveLuk R will probably not be effective for sampling purposes, unless you were to provide small batches, like one half gallon at a time, given on a daily basis.

LeveLuk JR II

The LeveLuk JRII is equipped with 3 large electrodes and produces Kangen® alkaline drinking water, clean water, Strong Kangen®, strong acidic and beauty water. Designed to produce all grades of water, while conserving energy. The pH range of the JRII is 2.5 – 11.5. The product comes with a 3-year warranty.

The JRII is an energy saving economy model. It is perfectly suited for use by an individual that does not travel far from the unit for any long periods of time. The power surging through the JRII is not as powerful as some of the other Enagic® models and it has fewer plates, so the properties of the water will not be as strong, or last as long.

NOTES:

LeveLuk SD501

The SD501 is equipped with 7 large electrodes and produces the best quality Kangen® alkaline drinking water, clean water, Strong Kangen®, strong acidic and beauty water available.

With the best automatic self-cleaning system in the industry and an average product life expectancy of over 20 years, it is no wonder this model is the top selling Enagic® unit. The pH range of the SD501 is 2.5 – 11.5. The product comes with a 5-year warranty.

The SD501 is the ionizer of choice for any medium – large family or for an Enagic® Distributor. Boasting 7 large plates and a robust power supply, the SD501 is able to create water with strong enough properties to give people samples. The length of time the properties of the water will last are dependent on the size and number of plates and the amount of power surging through them. The more plates and more power, the longer the properties last!

There is also an SD501 Platinum, which offers a stainless steel look to better blend in kitchens with stainless steel appliances. In addition to the stainless steel finish, the Platinum also offers operation voice prompts in 5 different languages, which include English, German, French, Italian and Spanish.

The SD501 model is also available in an under-the-counter configuration. This model must be installed by a qualified plumber or installation professional and requires a slightly different maintenance routine. I personally do not recommend the under the counter

NOTES:

model. Besides requiring additional maintenance, it also ends up being "hidden" and is not portable, so people will not be able to take it with them when they travel. If people are going to invest in the best quality water ionizer on the market, why in the world would they want to hide it? People should be encouraged to embrace the beauty of what this technology has to offer, as well as the way it looks.

LeveLuk K8

 The K8 is equipped with 8 large electrodes and produces Kangen® alkaline drinking water, clean water, Strong Kangen®, strong acidic and beauty water. Designed to produce all grades of water with longer lasting properties. The pH range of the K8 is 2.5 – 11.5. The product comes with a 5-year warranty.

The K8 is the latest machine introduced by Enagic and it is considered the "Hi-Tech" model, utilizing the most advanced technology and engineering. It produces all 7 grades of water and is more powerful than just about any other ionizer on the market, which allows it to produce water with long lasting properties!

It also features a state-of-the-art touch screen display and offers eight different language settings, including both visual and audio prompts.

NOTES:

Super 501

The Super 501 is equipped with a total of 12 large electrodes and produces top quality Kangen® alkaline drinking water, clean water, Strong Kangen®, strong acidic and beauty water.

Designed for high quantity water production, the Super 501 is a powerhouse and is the first and only water ionizer that comes with two separate electrolysis chambers. The pH range of the Super 501 is 2.5 – 11.5. The product comes with a 3-year warranty.

The Super 501 was built to handle frequent long term, continuous use. The strength of the 2.5 pH and 11.5 pH water right out of the machine is impressive and it is excellent for cleaning.

Enagic® Anespa DX

The Anespa DX is a unique mineral water generator. Equipped with a mineral ion water activator, the Anespa DX is able to moisturize the skin, make hair full and shiny and provide the relaxation of bathing in a natural hot spring.

The Anespa DX is the first product of its kind to use a twin cartridge system and is one of the most unique products in the Enagic® product line. The product comes with a 3-year warranty.

The Anespa DX is usually a secondary purchase. Most customers start with one of the Enagic® ionizers then,

NOTES:

once they start feeling the benefits from drinking Kangen Water®, they discover the additional, external benefits that can be created by using the Anespa DX.

These are the machines available as of the time this book was written. Understanding the differences between machines will allow you to find the right machine for each of your prospects. Enagic® also offers a nutritional supplement called Ukon®. You should find out more about this product as well, maybe even try it out!

SD501 Features & Waters

The SD501 is the #1 selling model in the Enagic® product line and, as such, it is important that you become familiar with the features and waters that it produces, since you will probably be selling more of these units than any other.

I would like to elaborate a bit on the differences between the units described in the previous section. Let's start by the real reason the SD501 is the #1 selling unit. Some people think that the SD501 is sold more often because it is the most expensive model, which would mean it would create the biggest commission for the seller. Unfortunately, this contention does not hold water, since the SD501 IS NOT the most expensive model!!

The Super 501 is the most expensive model. In fact, it is $2000.00 more than the SD501! So, if distributors were recommending machines based solely on which one would generate the highest commission, then the Super 501 would probably be the #1 selling model. But it is not!!

NOTES:

So, if it is not because it makes the sales person the most money, then why is the SD501 the top selling machine? Simply put, it is the model that meets the needs of the majority of users in this country. That is the bottom line and the real reason! Since the SD501 is the best seller, obviously it is important for you to learn as much as you can about this particular model. You should learn the basic specifications and the different grades of water that it produces.

There are only a few specifications that you really need to learn, but they are very important. The first is the number of plates, which is seven. These are large plates with a total surface area that is greater than just about any other ionizer on the market, even models that have more plates. You have to remember that total surface area is one of the most important factors in ionization.

The next important specification of the SD501 is the power supply. This model is one of the most powerful ionizers on the market and boasts an impressive maximum output of 230 Watts. The LeveLuk series of machines utilize a unique type of power supply in order to accomplish the extreme range of power outputs required of the machines.

In order to continuously generate Kangen Water, Strong Kangen Water and Strong Acidic Water, the highest quality Japanese circuits and engineering was needed. The result was a unique "hybrid" power configuration. The power supply utilizes a high quality SMPS, used to stabilize the electrical current, regardless of input fluctuation, while providing precision power output control, and a metal oxide semiconductor field-effect transistor, MOSFET, which is used for amplifying or switching electronic signals. This combination

NOTES:

- 53 -

increases efficiency, maximizes power output, reduces product weight and reduces the heat that a traditional transformer would create.

Once the electricity has passed through the SMPS and MOSFET, it is sent to a small transformer, where it is converted to a linear type of power; creating an even, consistent flow of electricity. This stable flow of power ionizes the water, regardless of duration or the power necessary to create the selected water. The best way to explain our power supply is as a hybrid, it's an SMPS with a Post Switch Transformer.

Another aspect of our design of the power supply is the sheer size of the heat sink, which helps cool the ionizer by absorbing and dissipating heat. It is the size of the entire power supply, and when it comes to heat sinks, size really does matter. The more surface area, to dissipate the heat generated, by continuously ionizing water, the better performance of your ionizer. It keeps the ionizer from overheating, which is a major problem for many of the other machines in the market.

The amounts of power surging through the plates are just as important as the plate size. These two factors are what ultimately create the beneficial properties of the water and will dictate how potent they are and, more importantly, how long they will last. The amount of time the properties will last is extremely important, especially if you are going to be sampling people the water.

Just on a side note, it is my opinion that the reason the competition does not sample their water is because the properties of the water produced by their machines is not strong enough or stable enough to be effective for days at a time. Sharing the Kangen Water® has been one of the most effective ways for us to sell and it only

NOTES:

makes sense that the competition would be doing the same thing, unless the water from their machines was ineffective for sampling.

The next specification of the SD501 that you should know is actually more of a feature, which is the Enhancer Tank. This is a feature that is completely downplayed, and even called unnecessary, by a lot of the competition. One thing that I have discovered in my experience in this industry is that if a competitor cannot match a feature of another machine, they will simply say it has no importance or even spin it as something negative.

Let me explain why the Enhancer Tank is very important and why the competition tries to lessen its value. Most of the other ionizers have the ability to produce water in a range between 3.0 – 3.5 pH and 10.5 – 11.0 pH. For the sake of argument and for this example, let's give them the benefit of the doubt and say that their machines are capable of producing 3.0 pH and 11.0 pH water. Each of these grades of water are much stronger than the neutral starting point of 7.0 pH. Based on the pH scale, the 3.0 pH water is 10,000 times more acidic than neutral, which sounds very impressive. And the 11.0 pH water is 10,000 times more alkaline than neutral, which also sounds quite impressive.

This is when the competition tries to say that their machines produce nearly the same grades of water and this is where the completion hopes consumers do not really understand the logarithmic nature of the pH scale. They will say that their machine produces water that is 3.0 pH and 11.0 pH and the Enagic® machines produce water that is 2.5 pH and 11.5 pH...that's hardly any difference at all! And they'd be right if we were talking about a simple progression of one more than the previous number. But we are not; we are talking about a progression of ten times more for each number.

This means that while the 3.0 pH water is 10,000 times more acidic than neutral, the 2.5 pH water is 50,000 times more acidic than neutral. And while the 11.0 pH water is 10,000 times more alkaline than neutral, the 11.5 pH water is 50,000 times more alkaline. Suddenly the minor difference in the strength and potency of the waters that the competition tries to trick consumers into believing becomes a huge difference!

The difference is in more than just the numbers, it is also in the way that the water can be used. Water with a pH level of 2.6 or less has been found to be very effective in killing a number of different bacteria. If the pH of the water is higher than 2.6 then the only thing that water will do to the bacteria is get it wet! The 11.5 pH water also has abilities that the 11.0 pH water does not have. The 11.5 pH water is so strong that it is able to break down certain oils. In some cases it is actually able to completely emulsify oil. This makes it a very effective cleaner and degreaser, without the need to use chemical based cleaners.

It is the Enhancer Tank, which contains a basic saline solution, which allows the SD501 to make these higher and lower pH grades of water. A small amount of the saline solution is injected into the electrolysis chamber during ionization, which results in the 2.5 pH and 11.5 pH waters.

Without the added saline solution, these waters would not be able to be made. Since none of the competition machines come with, or have an enhancer tank available as an option, they are unable to produce these levels of water. Again, since they cannot compete with this

NOTES:

feature of the SD501, they downplay the importance or try to imply that using a saline additive to make these grades of water is in some way a bad thing.

No matter what the competition might say, I can assure you that when you start using these grades of water to kill bacteria in your kitchen and remove oil based pesticides from your fresh fruits and vegetables, you will clearly recognize just how good that Enhancer Tank really is and so will your customers!!

These are probably the most important specifications / features of the SD501, so make sure you learn them and understand them! Next we will cover the different waters the SD501 produces.

But before we continue, I want to clarify some things about the name "Kangen Water®". As previously mentioned, "Kangen" does have an actual meaning. In Japanese the word "Kangen" translates to "Return to Origin", this is what the water is trying to help people achieve. This is also a trademarked name belonging to Enagic®. The name "Kangen Water®" refers to alkaline ionized drinking water which is produced by an Enagic® ionizer. Enagic® understands that the quality of their ionizers sets the water produced apart from that of other ionizers. As such, they decided to actually brand the water produced by their machines with its own name to identify and distinguish it from any other alkaline ionized drinking water. The intention was to establish "Kangen Water®" as the preferred alkaline ionized drinking water; so people can ask for it by name.

Many other companies have successfully used a brand name to identify a specific type of product. When you reach for a Kleenex, you are actually reaching for a tissue made by Kleenex. Have you ever made a Xerox

NOTES:

copy on a machine other than a Xerox? One of the most widely recognized is the Band-Aid brand. Their brand has become so well known that most people refer to any adhesive bandage as a "Band-Aid". Following suit with these iconic brands, Enagic® is working diligently to ensure that when people in this market ask for the best alkaline water available, that they ask for it by name, "Kangen Water®"!

Kangen Water® – The SD501 produces three grades of alkaline drinking water: 8.5 pH, 9.0 pH and 9.5 pH. These pH values represent alkaline levels that are 50, 100 and 500 times stronger than neutral. How acidic a person is will determine which level of water they should be drinking in order to balance their overall body pH. Because of lifestyle choices and diet, some people are closer to being balanced, so they only need the 8.5 pH level; while others are more acidic and need the 9.5 pH Kangen Water®.

Clean Water – This is filtered water that has not gone through the ionization process for those taking prescription medications. Some time-release medications can dissolve quicker than intended as a result of the micro-clustering property of ionized water. As a precaution, Enagic® recommends that all prescription medications be taken with Clean Water.

Beauty Water – This is water with a pH level of 4.0 – 6.5 and is not intended for drinking. The main use of this water is for topical application to the skin. The pH level is slightly more acidic than the skin, which allows it to tone and tighten. This water is also excellent for certain types of cooking, including boiling pasta and beans.

Strong Acidic Water – This is water with a pH level of 2.6 or less and is not intended for drinking. With the ability

NOTES:

to thoroughly sterilize and sanitize it is perfectly suited for use in any area where contaminants may be found, including kitchens and restrooms. It can also be used to clean foods that may have been exposed to bacteria, including fresh produce and poultry. It is also a very effective hand sanitizer when used to wash hands before food preparation or after handling foods.

Strong Kangen Water® – This is water with a pH level of 11.5 or higher and is not intended for drinking. This is water that is strong enough to emulsify oil, but can be used to clean foods of all kinds, including fresh produce and fish. It is also an excellent all-purpose cleaner, with incredible degreasing abilities. It can also be used to blanch and pre-boil certain vegetables.

The different grades of water produced by the SD501 have many more uses than those listed, but these will give you a starting point when talking to your prospects about the different uses of the water. Enagic® has put together a comprehensive guide to different ways to use each grade of water called "The Advantages Of Using Electrolytic Water" and is included in the information package that accompanies each machine.

I highly recommend that you find this valuable information and that you review it and then try out some of the suggested ways to use the water. I think you will find the waters produced by the SD501 have many more uses than you ever thought possible and that you will discover the SD501 is an amazing piece of technology!

NOTES:

The "Competition"

I will tell you right off the bat that many of you may not like the way that I am going to explain the competition, because I am not going to address specific companies or brands of ionizers. Instead, I am going to take more of a generic, generalized approach and explain overall aspects of the competition. The main reason I am not going to address any specific company or model is because, as you will soon discover, the vast majority of the "different" competition machines are not really all that different. In fact, roughly 85% of the competition ionizers, which represents about 15 different brands and about 25 different models, are actually manufactured in the exact same Korean factory.

The reality is that you really don't need to know about specific brands or models; once you learn about the "features" that most of them have in common you can

NOTES:

address the shortcomings of almost all of the competition machines.

The other reason I am not going to address specific companies is because they might not even be in business by the time this edition is printed, so what would be the point of naming names and pointing fingers? Just in the last year we have seen several companies go from "creating a buzz" to complete obscurity. In one instance a so-called "major" competitor ceased to exist entirely after less than a year in the limelight.

I have thoroughly researched the other companies and ionizers and have found some pretty interesting information. But before we dive into the competition, please allow me to provide a "Readers Digest" version of the history of ionizers and the competition.

Ionization experiments date back all the way to the late 1700's, but the modern process of ionization was advanced by Russian scientists over 60 years ago. Them in the 1950's the Japanese started working with the technology for application on living things and began to develop machines that were initially introduced in commercial applications, primarily in hospitals.

Jump ahead about 35 years and the technology had progressed to the point that much smaller, consumer versions were being made. These consumer models were originally produced and introduced in Japan. About 7 years later a company in Korea started to produce a scaled down, cheaper version of the original ionizer.

I don't know if you are familiar with the term "Reversed Engineered" but that is basically what happened with

NOTES: _____

this technology. Japanese versions of the technology were taken to Korea, where they were disassembled, basically taking it apart to see how it was made.

By taking the finished product apart, they were able to figure out how to build a similar product. Then tooling and manufacturing is figured out and like products begin to be made. Typically these products are of lower quality and they often use the strength and reputation of the original product to help sell their version of it.

Today there are basically three different types of companies in the water ionizer industry operating in the U.S. and abroad: Manufacturers, Private Label Manufacturers and Resellers. Enagic® is really the only "Manufacturer" operating globally today, meaning that they actually manufacture their own brand of ionizers and the sales & service are actually handled by them as well. This is very important because it illustrates the level of commitment the company has to the product and the industry.

If you are not actually making a product, it is very easy to walk away from it if things slow down or if you just don't feel like representing that product any more. When you manufacture a product and provide all the support, it means that you have committed to the product for the long haul. Tens of millions of dollars have been invested in research and development; in manufacturing tooling and machinery; in facilities and staff; in warranty and support. These are just a few of the things that really make the difference when you are a full service manufacturer, the difference between Enagic® and the competition!

After an actual manufacturer are the "Private Label Manufacturers". These are companies which build

NOTES: _____

ionizers, but they primarily do so for other companies. They don't normally build ionizers which reflect their own company name or brand. This is the only time I will mention any another company by name, because I think it is extremely important that, as a distributor, you are familiar with these companies.

Dong Yang Science Co. Ltd., is based in Korea, but they also conduct marketing and sales operations under the names Emco Tech & Royal Water. They build machines for about 10 different brands. There are slight differences in features and design, but the core technology is exactly the same and over 95% of the actual components of these machines are identical.

There are a bunch of different "brands" which are nothing more than the exact same technology and components, just with a different name. These include Jupiter, IonWays, AlkaViva, Echo and others. While these machines have a sticker with a different brand name on the front of the ionizers they sell, when they talk about "their" ionizers, they are referring to models that are actually Dong Yang machines.

Another important point about the private label brands is that the actual manufacturer does not provide service support for the machines; it is provided by a company that usually has no real experience or expertise in ionizer repair and maintenance, they mainly sell them. Dong Yang has no branches here in the U.S., so there is no way to get local support from the company that actually manufactured the machine. Obviously this is a huge drawback for anyone purchasing one of these machines.

The last groups are the "Resellers". These are independent sellers that are authorized to sell and

NOTES:

- 63 -

distribute here in the U.S. on behalf of the company, most of which are in Korea. There are currently 2 or 3 main resellers operating in the U.S. Again, these are not the manufacturers and support / service is only available while these companies are in business.

We recently saw an example of what happens to consumers when one of these resale companies goes under. There use to be a resale company operating here in the U.S. that is no longer in business. Now any previous customer of this company has no support or service available at all. They can't even get a replacement filter once their old one needs to be replaced.

The core technology and components used by these companies are pretty much the same as the other Korean companies. There is a lot more detailed information about the competition out there, but this at least gives you a basic understanding of these other ionizer companies. As for the other products, the bottom line is that they are less expensive for a reason, which is quality and output, nothing more!

Really, don't you think that these other companies would sell their machines for more money if they could? Does it not stand to reason that if these machines were actually the same and if people were willing to pay more that they would charge more? These other machines cost less because they are worth less...period!

Spin Masters – The majority of our competition are virtual, Internet based resellers that I refer to as "Spin Masters". These are people that can turn babble into benefit; flaws into features; garbage into gold. Their expertise is convincing consumers that an inferior

NOTES:

product is superior by spinning the truth or by redirection.

You see, while these people may be devious, they are not stupid.   In fact, they are very cunning and calculating in their approach and they have a systematic way that they do things.   This is what they do for a living.

You have to understand that there is a lot of psychology and emotional manipulation employed by these resellers. They've worked very hard to develop a way to manipulate information and utilize emotional response in order to sway people to purchase their products.   If you took a no-nonsense, common sense look at the competition from the perspective of a consumer, there would be no way that someone would purchase their products, and they know it!

This is why they engage in spinning their product features, redirecting emphasis on price instead of benefit and attacking method of market introduction instead of product quality and performance. They know that this is what they have to do in order to effectively sell their machines.

The best way to protect against this is to warn your prospects of what they will be facing when they go on the Internet to find out more.   You have to realize that there is a very fine line between "slamming" the competition and warning prospects of the misinformation and redirection they will find online, so try not to cross that line.

Informing your prospects of what they will find is fine, in fact it is your responsibility to let them know so they do not fall victim to these campaigns.   Just don't let your

NOTES:

informing turn into bad mouthing or berating the competition. That is basically stooping to their level, which we do not need to do, as we have a superior product.

I addressed this in the *60 Second Internet Expert* section of the book, but I think this is important enough to go into it a little deeper. Here are examples of the two approaches: informing and slamming.

Informing: "Now that you know a little more about the water I figure that you will do your due diligence and find out even more by doing some Internet research, I know I would. I just want to warn you about some of the things you might find. You see, our company has become very successful by offering the best ionizers available and whenever you're the best other products try to copy you and say they are just as good. As consumers we see it in advertising all the time. Well, unfortunately, our product is no different and we've found being the best comes at a price. Let me just warn you about what you might run into. First, you may come across a website that looks like an unbiased, consumer review site, that promotes itself as the "authority" to turn to when looking for an ionizer. Just so you are aware, there are no unbiased websites that have reviewed ionizers. Consumer Reports has not yet done a review on ionizers and all the other sites are owned or operated by an ionizer company or distributor. Second, you may run into one of the smear campaigns initiated by the competition. Basically these are campaigns embedded into search results that try to convince consumers that the price difference of our products and theirs are because the way the products are sold, not because ours are superior products. I know you are a savvy consumer and that you would not fall for that, but I figure I should at least mention it. I think it is funny that they would blatantly insult the intelligence of consumers by insinuating that a company could stay in business for over 40 years selling an overpriced product. We all know that an overpriced product could never survive for that long in a retail market! The last thing you might run into is the competition "spins". This is when the competition starts doing component comparisons between their products and ours. They take what we would consider design flaws and try to turn them into features and I will give them this, they are pretty good at it! They have been able to take some real negatives and make them almost sound impressive. But, again, I feel that they are insulting consumers by employing this strategy. Consumers know when a company starts comparing their product to another one, that theirs is inferior and the one being compared to is the superior product; we've all known this since products started doing comparisons. Yet they do it anyway. These are a few things that I wanted to warn you about so that you don't get distracted or misled during your own research."

Yes, this seems like a lot, and it is! Believe it or not, once you have said this a few times, you can run though just about all of it in just a couple of minutes. It will take time for you to get to the point that you can convey all this information quickly, but that time will come. Please do not try to use the above as a script to recite to prospects, just use it as a guide of the type of information you will want to warn them about as they take the next step in the exposure process.

Now here is an example of "slamming" the competition.

Slamming: "Just in case you decide to go onto the Internet I want to warn you about what you will find. There are these fake product review websites that are

NOTES:

nothing but a bunch of lies. Each site is owned by the company that gets the best review. They just say that their product is the best and that ours are just okay, they are just a bunch of liars. Then there are these smear campaigns that say that the only reason that our products are priced so high is because they company pays distributors to sell the products. It's just a bunch of lies and these guys are a bunch of scum bags. Then they attack our products saying that theirs have better features and are priced lower. They are just a bunch of liars, so don't believe what they say."

Taking the slamming approach can actually be counterproductive. Calling the competition liars makes you sound petty and unprofessional; besides, there are ways to alluded to the fact that someone is dishonest without calling them a liar! In taking the "slamming" approach you might actually end up planting seeds or ideas that will end up benefiting the competition.

In my example I said, "...there are these smear campaigns that say that the only reason that our products are priced so high is because the company pays distributors to sell the products..." I have heard people say this exact thing. I don't think they realized that by saying this they are actually the ones that planted the idea of our products being overpriced because distributors are getting paid.

You have to be very careful what you say and how you say it, as it is very easy convey the wrong message. It is much better to be professional and provide information instead of just criticism.

When dealing with the competition it really boils down to understanding the three main things that influence the creation of ionized water, which are total surface

NOTES:

area of the electrodes (plates), amount of time the water is in contact with the electrodes and the amount of power surging through the electrodes. These are the three factors that will determine the strength of the properties of the water and how long they will last. This is one of the most important aspects of our machines and the reason that we are able to sample our water.

The following are the main so-called "features" that the competition has put their "spin" on to make them sound like positive selling points instead of the product weaknesses that they actually are. These are the things that you will want to really learn how to explain to prospects, if and when the topic arises. If you know the how's and why's of the engineering of the competitors' products it becomes much easier to deal with the topic.

Mesh Plate Electrodes: In theory a flat surface with holes in it could actually create a greater amount of total surface area than that of a solid surface. The catch is that the plate would have to be very thick in order to actually accomplish this, which is just not the case when it comes to the mesh plate electrodes in the majority of the competition machines.

If you see one of these plates you will discover that they are practically paper thin and that the connection that passes electricity to the plate is just a flimsy post wedged into some of the mesh screen and sticking off of the side. I think it is an important part of every distributor's education to make sure they at least see a picture of a mesh plate, compared to a plate from an Enagic® ionizer. If at all possible they should try to see and feel an actual plate from one of these machines. Doing so will remove all doubt that mesh plates are in any way superior to the solid plates used in the Enagic® machines.

NOTES:

These plates are touted as being superior and more efficient, when nothing could be further from the truth. They reduce cost, which is why they are used. At the thickness of these plates the holes do not increase the surface area, if anything the surface area is decreased as a result of the mesh plates. These types of plates are less expensive to manufacture and to plate with the platinum, which is why they are used...period!

The following is a quote from a competitor's website talking about mesh plate electrodes; this is where they put their "spin" regarding mesh plates: "...five of the most advanced mesh platinum-titanium electrodes in the world...the electrodes are covered in a "super fine" mesh with very distinct high points and valleys..."

After extensive investigation and research it was discover that the "distinct high points and valleys" were, in fact, nothing more than holes. But what a spin!! They took the fact that their plates have holes in them and turned it into an impressive sounding feature that would fool even the savviest of consumers!

Auto Heat Shut Off Sensor: This is one of my favorite spins, because it is just so ridiculous! This particular "feature" will be called slightly different things depending on the brand. It may be an "over heat detector", or a "high temperature overload" or a "temperature sensor / auto shut off".

And sometimes they will use very impressive verbiage to try to make it sound even more impressive. This is an actual quote from a competitor's website: "High Temperature Overload: Automatic transthermal temperature sensor shutoff and reset protection". Sounds impressive! But no matter what they are called, they all do the same

NOTES:

thing, which is shut down the flow of electricity to the electrodes if the machine starts to overheat.

Now, let's consider this "feature" from a consumer perspective, but let's put it in a context that may be more familiar to the American Consumer...automobiles. So, let's say that you buy a new car and after driving it for a little while the temperature starts to go up, then without warning, it reaches a hot enough temperature that the car automatically turns itself off, thus avoiding any severe damage that may be caused from overheating.

If you have ever been driving a car and had it die, you know what a nightmare that can be; imagine if the car dying was actually intentional, it's a scary thought. Now, seriously, if this scenario happened to you, would you keep this car or would you take it to the dealership to demand your money back or to at least demand that they fix the overheating problem? Honestly, could you, even for a second, ever believe that a car automatically shutting off when it gets to hot is somehow a benefit? You wouldn't think so, yet people are duped by this spin in the ionizer industry all the time!

Dual Filters: This is another great spin, because it would seem that two would be better than one. It makes sense, until you understand why there are two filters. You see, the filter of an ionizer is supposed to remove impurities and make the water as pristine as possible before entering the electrolysis chamber.

This should be able to be accomplished using a single filter. So why is it that some other ionizers have dual filters? The reason may surprise you. It is to put stuff IN the water, not take it out.

NOTES:

To fully appreciate why this is being done you really do need to understand some of the fundamentals of ionization. The main thing you need to know is that in order to ionize water through electrolysis there must be minerals present in the water. These act as conductors for the electrical charge. The more minerals in the water, the greater the conductivity; the greater the conductivity, the greater the ionization.

Because the makers of many of these other machines know that the power surging through their machine is not sufficient to ionize with the mineral content that is found in most tap water, they add additional minerals into the water from the second filter, which creates a slightly stronger charge.

Some of these minerals also have a higher pH level, so, when tested with pH drops, the water will appear to have a higher alkaline level than if it solely went off the pH created from ionization without the "extras". Using additives to boost the pH level kind of defeats the whole purpose of ionizing the water, which is to effectively use the mineral content that is found in the source water to maximize the splitting of alkaline and acidic water that is inherent in the water.

One more issue that can be created by the introduction of these added minerals into the electrolysis chamber is over calcification. One of the most popular minerals that are used in the second filter of these dual filter machines is calcium. When water passes through the second filter additional calcium is released into the water. While this will increase the conductivity of the source water, it will also allow even more calcium to build up in the machine.

NOTES:

- 72 -

In case I have not mentioned it before, mineral build up is the KILLER of these machines, which is the main reason that you should make sure your machine is cleaned often. To actually add more calcium to already hard water makes no sense at all. The slight benefit that may be created from the added conductivity does not justify the potential harm being inflicted on the machine.

Auto Flow Control Sensor: This is another masterfully spun "feature" of many of the other ionizers. And, again, in order to truly appreciate the spin, you have to understand some basics about ionization. Remember the three main factors that will influence the quality of the water produced by an ionizer: power, plate size, and length of time the water is in physical contact with the plate.

Since the designers of these other machines know that they have lower powered machines and much smaller total plate surface area, they have devised a way to manipulate the flow of water so that they can force longer contact with the plates. The "auto flow control" is nothing more than a built in regulator that limits the physical amount of water that can pass through the machine at any one time.

With an auto flow control sensor, which is connected to a control valve, it would not matter how high you were to turn on your faucet, because the valve would control the flow once the water actually entered the machine.

With the flow reduced the water pressure is less and the water passes over the plates slower and in less volume. This results in the water having higher "out of the machine" readings, but the properties are very unstable and dissipate very quickly.

NOTES:

The auto flow control is one of the main reasons that the other ionizers take so long to produce any real quantity of ionized water. The flow rate is typically one-third to one-half that of our machines. The amount of power and the large plate size are what allow our machines to be able to operate without this type of flow control. This is just one more design flaw that the competition spins into what they consider a product feature.

As you can see the competition has taken a lot of time to develop their spins and they are more than ready to try to spin your prospects from the best ionizer on the market to what they have to offer.

It is your job to protect your prospect by knowing how the competition spins things and by warning your prospects of what they will find. Don't be afraid of the competition, because, really, we don't have any competition, we just have other companies that happen to sell other ionizers.

Always remember that the reason we are able to provide people with samples of the water is because our machines can produce properties that are strong enough to last for several days.

Also remember that the reason that the competition has not followed our lead with sampling people their water is because their machines do not produce water with strong enough properties to last several days, which is the only reason they do not sample their water. They can say whatever they want; the bottom line is that their water does not have the properties to support sampling!

Educate yourself to the differences between what they have to offer and what we have to offer and recognize that there truly is a difference! Remember, when you

NOTES:

"think" something, there is room for doubt, but when you "know" something, you become bullet proof!

Know that the other ionizers have major design flaws. Know that the sellers of these other ionizers will do and say almost anything to procure a sale. Know that your prospects deserve the best value and product for their money. Know that our ionizers produce the longest lasting and most beneficial properties. Know that you represent the best ionizers on the market. Don't just think these things...KNOW THEM!!

Now that you know more about the competition and their product "features" I am going to address one more thing regarding the competition, which is why they work so hard to use the efforts of Enagic® Distributors to sell their own products. The answer is easy, they engage in what is referred to as "Predatory Marketing", meaning that they create marketing and advertising campaigns that prey on prospects created by someone else's efforts.

You see, because most of these other ionizer sellers have so little at risk, they are not willing to put much into actually trying to procure their own customers. They rely on trickery, deception, high pressure sales techniques and manipulation of emotional response to get consumers to purchase their products.

Most people don't truly understand just how much time and money it takes a company to turn a consumer into one of their customers. In marketing this is referred to as "Cost of Customer Acquisition", meaning how much money a company actually has to spend in order to earn the business of a customer.

NOTES:

Most of these other ionizer companies are not willing or able to invest the substantial amounts of money necessary to develop and secure their own customer base. Instead, they use every underhanded technique they can come up with in order to get one or our prospects to stumble across their product information.

They are not taking the time and money needed to develop a sales force that can educate consumers in this new market about this unfamiliar technology. They do not embark on major campaigns to PROVE to consumers that the product they have to offer is really the best one available.

They wait until an unsuspecting prospect gets tangled in their web of Internet based misinformation and deceit and then they strike! These types of tactics are really the only way they can compete with the quality of our products, which is why they will never go head to head with us. They may post biased reviews, comparisons and even manipulated "laboratory" results...but the reality is that if the top five brands on the market were to go head to head against the SD501, under IDENTICAL testing conditions and testing protocols, the SD501 would emerge as the undisputed champion!

It is this major difference in quality that leads us to another major difference in marketplace introduction, which is our ability to bring this technology to the commercial market. You see, the competition may be able to dupe an average consumer, but it is much more difficult to pull the wool over the eyes of a business customer. The scrutiny made by a commercial customer is much greater; as the purchase affects more than just them...it may also affect their customers and livelihood. It is for this reason that most of the other companies do not even bother trying to approach commercial accounts, they know that what they have to offer simply cannot stand up to the rigorous requirements of commercial use.

On the other hand, the Enagic® products are more than able to stand up to the intense scrutiny and expectations of commercial applications, which leads us to the next bonus section in this Second Edition of Ride The Wave: Targeted Markets. But before we dive into some of the specific targeted markets, let's take a quick look at some of the important certifications which allow the Enagic® products to be used commercially.

We will start at the beginning of the product process, which is manufacturing. The quality of manufacturing tells a lot about the ultimate quality of the product. If a product undergoes rigorous quality control and standards during manufacturing, it is reasonable to assume that the end product will be reflective of those expectations. However, the adverse is also true, meaning that if the manufacturing of a product is sub-standard, you will most likely end up with a lower quality product.

Well, Enagic® adheres to the highest manufacturing standards and quality control in the entire industry, which, not surprisingly, is one of the main reasons they make the best water ionizers. Now it would be very easy for any company to tell a consumer that they manufacture their products under strict quality guidelines, but it is something entirely different when an unbiased, third party is the one making the claims. This is exactly what Enagic® has and exactly what the competition does not have!

There is a non-profit organization called the International Organization of Standardization, also known as ISO, which that has created guidelines for companies that manufacture products. It is not a requirement that any company adhere to these guidelines, but it should be noted that the biggest and the best in the manufacturing industry DO adhere to these standards and that ISO Certification is something that they proudly promote when they have earned the distinction to do so.

It is important to note that Enagic® not only adheres to these standards, but that their manufacturing plant has been inspected and that have earned a number of different ISO certifications. They have ISO9001, which is certification for compliance of manufacturing quality. This means that Enagic® meets or exceeds the requirements set forth by the ISO for the quality of their products. There are a few other ionizer manufacturers that also have an ISO9001 certification, but, at least as of the date of that this manuscript is being written, it is the only one that any other ionizer company has. Enagic® actually has quite a few others.

There are two more that I want to take the time to mention, because I think they are VERY important. The first is ISO 14001, which is certification for environmental compliance. This means that Enagic® meets or exceeds the ISO requirements for impact on the environment during the manufacturing process. Enagic® has often claimed to be an environmentally friendly company and this ISO Certification clearly supports those claims! If you care about the environment, you should make sure that the ionizer company that you will give your business has ISO14001 Certification!

The last ISO certification we will cover may just be the most important. It is the ISO 13485, which is

NOTES:

certification for producing medical grade products. This means that the Enagic® manufacturing plant has been inspected and has passed the requirements set forth by the ISO to receive this distinction. I think that it is VERY important to note that NO OTHER ionizer company has this ISO certification! This alone should speak volumes as to the quality of the products produced by Enagic®. Maybe even more important is that it speaks volumes about the quality, or lack thereof, of the products produced by other companies that do not meet or exceed, or even attempt, to adhere to manufacturing standards that would earn them this certification!

Dealing with an ISO Certified company is one more way that consumers can be assured that the products they are purchasing are the best. Consumers should be encouraged to learn more about the importance if ISO Certification and they should be educated about what those certifications really mean to them...which are quality products, offered by a quality company!

The next certification we will discuss is one of the most important, especially for commercial application. This is NSF / ANSI certification. These are certifications that address specific requirements that are imposed by agencies like the Health Department. They are to ensure that products used in businesses like restaurants meet or exceed the requirements necessary when providing things that people eat or drink. Requirements like these are what have helped greatly reduce the rate of food borne illness, also known as food poisoning.

One of the biggest non-profit governing bodies of the water industry is the Water Quality Association, the WQA. They provide testing and certification services that are used by the biggest and most respected companies in the water industry.

NOTES:

In addition to being Members of the WQA, Enagic® has also undergone the rigorous and demanding review and testing process for WQA Gold Seal Certification. It is important to note that this distinction has been issued for the entire Enagic® LeveLuk series of ionizers.

Enagic has been granted WQA Gold Seal NSF / ANSI 42 Certification, which means that "a production model of the listed line of drinking water treatment units was tested at the Water Quality Association laboratory, or any of the other testing laboratories recognized by the Water Quality Association, and was found to have met the standards for reduction of specific aesthetic-related contaminants in drinking water. In addition, the materials and components used in these certified drinking water treatment units have met the rigorous safety and structural integrity and strength requirements set by industry Standard NSF/ANSI-42."

Enagic has also been granted WQA Gold Seal NSF / ANSI 372 Certification for lead reduction. The following is the description of this certification by the WQA: "Certification to NSF/ANSI 372 (Previously, WQA's Other Recognized Document (ORD), ORD0902), was established by WQA to compile the minimum requirements for the evaluation of lead content in drinking water products, material, and components for compliance to laws, regulations, or other restrictions for lead content. NSF/ANSI 372 combines the lead content calculations from NSF/ANSI 61 — Annex G and the testing protocol established by the California Department of Toxic Substances. Certification to NSF/ANSI 372 demonstrates compliance to the following: • California Health and Safety Code Section 116875 definition of "lead free" (A.K.A. NSF/ANSI 61 – Annex G, AB 1953), and • Vermont's lead in consumer products law, 9 V.S.A., Chapter 63, Subchapter 1C, and •

NOTES:

Any other law, regulation, or restriction on lead content that may use the same calculations and testing protocol to demonstrate "lead free" compliance."

Enagic water ionizers also have WQA certification, CSAB483.1, is for product performance and is defined by the WQA as meaning "a production model of the listed line of drinking water treatment units was tested at the Water Quality Association laboratory, or any of the other testing laboratories recognized by the Water Quality Association, and was found to have met the applicable performance requirements found in the standard. In addition, the materials and components used in these certified drinking water treatment units have met the rigorous safety and structural integrity and strength requirements set by industry Standard CSA B483.1."

The latest, and perhaps most significant, NSF / ANSI certification that Enagic has earned is the NSF / ANSI 18 Certification, for manual food and beverage dispensing equipment. "This Standard contains requirements for equipment and devices that manually dispense food or beverages, in bulk or in portions. The materials, design, and construction requirements of this Standard may also be applied to an item that is manufactured as a component of food and beverage dispensing equipment." This certification is specifically focused for use in a commercial environment.

It is VERY IMPORTANT to note that, as of the date that this manuscript is being written, Enagic® is the ONLY water ionizer manufacturer IN THE WORLD that has earned and been granted the coveted these WQA Gold Seal Certifications. NO other water ionizer has all of these certifications and no other ionizer is certified to be used for commercial application. This is one more

NOTES:

honor, in a long list of honors and distinctions, which sets the Enagic® water ionizers apart from any other brand. Enagic® products ARE the gold standard in the industry! Enagic®... the proof is in the water... everything else is just talk!

I want to make something VERY clear to every distributor that reads this book...WE ARE ALWAYS GOING TO HAVE OTHER PRODUCTS OUT THERE COMPETING WITH OURS AND WE ARE ALWAYS GOING TO HAVE TO DEFEND OURSELVES AGAINST THEIR ATTACKS, COMPARISONS AND CRITICISM. This goes along with being the best in an industry.

The following is something I'd like to share with you to illustrate this point, it is called the *Penalty of Leadership*, written by Theodore MacManus.

In every field of human endeavor, he that is the leader in his field must perpetually live in the white light of publicity. Whether the leadership be vested in a man or in a manufactured product, emulation and envy are ever at work.

In art, in literature, in music, in industry, the reward and the punishment are always the same. The reward is widespread recognition; the punishment, fierce denial and detraction. When a man's work becomes a standard for the whole world, it also becomes a target for the shafts of the envious few. If his work is mediocre, he will be left severely alone – if he achieves a masterpiece, it will set a million tongues a-wagging.

Jealousy does not protrude its forked tongue at the artist who produces a commonplace painting. Whatsoever you write, or paint, or play, or sing, or build, no one will strive to surpass or to slander you unless your work is stamped with the seal of genius. The leader is attacked because he is a leader, and the effort to equal him is merely added proof of that leadership.

NOTES:

Failing to equal or to surpass, the follower seeks to depreciate and to destroy – but only confirms once more the superiority of that which he strives to deny. There is nothing new in this. It is as old as the world and as old as human passions – envy, fear, greed, ambition, and the desire to surpass. And it all avails nothing.

If the leader truly leads, he remains – the leader. Master-poet, master-painter, master-craftsman, each in his turn is attacked, and each holds his achievements throughout the ages. That which is good or great makes itself known, no matter how loud the clamor of denial. That which deserves to live – lives.

This text appeared as an ad for the Cadillac Motor Car Company in the Saturday Evening Post in 1915. The things we are experiencing with our so-called "competition" is nothing new; this is what happens when you are the best. The reality is that our competition will come and go, but like you just read, *"That which deserves to live – lives…"*, and while I can't say this about our competition, without a doubt, Enagic WILL LIVE!!

On an ironic side note, it just so happens that, out of ALL the other car makes and models, the 2014 Cadillac CTS Sedan was voted the Motor Trend 2014 Car of the Year. It won't surprise me a bit if, in 2074, after 100 years in business, Enagic is still recognized as the Leader and Gold Standard in this industry. Cadillac did it and I know Enagic can too!

NOTES:

Get Trained & Independent ASAP!

One of the keys to success as an Independent Enagic® Distributor is to break free from depending on others as quickly as possible. The best and most effective way to do this is to get trained and learn how to do this business yourself.

While it is great to have a supportive sponsor, your ultimate goal is to become self-sufficient as fast as you can. This is important for a couple of reasons. First, if you are depending on someone else for your success, then you end up on their schedule for your success! I don't know about you, but I do not like having someone else controlling how and when my success happens. I like to have as much control over that as possible! The other reason it is important for you to become independent as quickly as possible is because what you do will end up being what you teach.

Ask yourself this, would you want a bunch of distributors relying on you for their success? Or would you like to help them become independent as soon as possible, so they can fly on their own? Your answer should be to have them fly on their own, because you have to remember that as your distributors succeed, so do you!! By setting the example of how to become independent, you empower your distributors to take action and to then teach their team members how to do the same thing! Your distributors are kind of like acorns...they have the potential for greatness, but if they don't get some help, they are just another nut going nowhere!

NOTES:

The easiest way to become independent is to seek out as much training as possible. Something that most people do not understand is that training is more of a frame of mind then an actual event. Of course, there are training events, but the effectiveness of any training really boils down to the person attending the training.

If you want your business to grow from the little acorn to the mighty oak, I suggest that you try to turn every exposure in the Enagic® business into a training opportunity for you and your team members.

NOTES:

Now if you apply that mind set to everything you do with the Enagic® business, you will be up to speed very quickly. Make every exposure your own personal training. Become a sponge and soak up as much as you can. Go to as many presentations, demos, luncheons, meetings, etc. as possible. Each holds a new lesson just waiting for you to learn it!!

Of course, you will also want to seek out actual training opportunities. A few that you should try to tap into are the Kangen1 Direct Distributor Training, the Leadership Development Seminars, any of the Kangen1 Power Training Events and, of course, any Enagic events. These are very effective trainings and can really accelerate your success.

Another great way to get trained is to attend events with your own team members. When you do this you are both getting training that will ultimately help you build your business. Again, if you lead by example and attend trainings, instead of just promoting them, you will develop a much stronger business and much more effective and independent distributors. Those little acorns you helped along the way will develop into Mighty Oaks!

NOTES:
_____

Goal Setting

For most people, a goal is a general idea instead of a specific destination. It is a poorly thought out wish, instead of a concrete direction. Saying that you want to make a lot of money or buy a big house, these are not goals, these are really nothing more than wishes, and unless you have a genie in a bottle, wishes don't really amount to very much. Without actual goals, you don't know what actions are necessary to turn them from wishes to reality.

What is a "Goal"...it is your destination. The place you're trying to get to, from where you are right now. That place may be represented by a number of different things: a certain level of income, a new car, a new address, a college fund for your child, additional money for your church or favorite charity, it can be anything you want it to be, as long as it is an actual goal. It needs to be specific, without specifics you can't identify the final destination. And you have to write your goals down on paper. This is very important! Until a goal is written on paper, it is just a notion, an intangible idea. Putting your goals on paper makes it real, it gives the notion substance, it goes from simply an idea or thought, to something that exists!

The easiest way to understand goals is to think about them in familiar terms. Let's look at setting goals in the same way you would map out a cross-country trip. If you are going cross-country, you wouldn't simply walk out the door of your house, jump your car and start driving. Even the most spontaneous of people, would need to make some type of preparation. Some type of plan in order to reach their desired destination. Obviously, in order to plan a trip we need to know where we're going. This is why, when setting goals, you have to start with the ultimate destination. Starting with the destination will allow us to figure out what we need to do to get there.

Let's say we're in Los Angeles, California and we want to travel to New York City, New York. By establishing our specific destination, which is New York City, we can now figure out what it will take to make the trip.

Just like setting goals, there's a lot more to it than simply grabbing the map and taking off. There are many factors involved, things that must be taken into consideration, in order to successfully make the journey and reach the destination. We need a map to help guide us along the way. But we also need to know where we can get gas, where we can get food, where the restrooms are, where we can sleep and many other factors. These are all the incidentals that are necessary in order to make this a successful trip.

Goal setting is the same way. Where you want to end up will dictate where your journey will take you, where you will need to stop along the way and the things you will need to help you get to your destination. And just like our road trip, goals have to be broken into smaller pieces so that they are manageable. Our ultimate destination represents our long-term goal. The first stop in the leg of the journey would represent a short-term goal. When you're setting your goals, you want to make sure you do the same thing.

Setting short-term goals allows you to monitor and make sure that you are headed in the right direction to your ultimate destination. In our cross-country trip we would have a number of stops along the way. Each one of those stops would represent a short-term goal that we had accomplished. By accomplishing each of these

NOTES:

short-term goals, we come closer and closer to our desired destination. Having these short-term goals gives us the opportunity to stay on track and puts us closer to achieving our long-term goal, while at the same time keeping the journey from becoming overwhelming and seemingly impossible.

The other aspect of goal setting that many people overlook is that setting goals will actually allow you to create a game plan of what you need to do to accomplish those goals. Knowing your goal gives you the ability to create a plan of action. Without knowing your destination, it is much more difficult to figure out what you need to do in order to get there.

Once you establish your goals, you can figure out what you'll need to do on a quarterly, monthly, weekly and even daily basis in order to achieve them. Every distributor in this project has the ability to create a formula that will specifically let them know what they need to do in order to meet their goals. However, in order to do this, the first thing a person needs to do is take this business seriously and treat it like a business.

The formula for each distributor is very different. It is based on personal effort, ability, drive, determination, focus and many other things. For this reason I really can't give you a specific example of how to do it. What I can say is this; to create your formula all you have to do is identify your long-term goal. Let's say this is a dollar figure that you want to earn after one year. Based on that dollar figure you can calculate what you will need to do in order to achieve that goal.

Even as a brand-new distributor, you will quickly be able to identify how much specific effort goes into making a sale. This effort will be comprised of how many people you have to talk to, how much water you have to sample and the number of meetings you will to have to attend with your prospects. Once you have those numbers, you can calculate exactly what you will need to do in order to meet your goals.

There are some variables, like which distributors in your group will help you get to your goal faster, that you may not be able to immediately identify. However, identifying the necessary actions for you to personally meet your goals will give you a foundation to work from. If you are detailed enough, you can actually figure out how many gallons of water you'll need to get out and how many new prospects you'll need to talk to on a daily basis.

If you are a brand-new distributor, meaning that you have not yet made your first product sale, then your first goal is very simple. Make your first personal product sale. This would be your initial short-term goal. Once you accomplish this, your second short-term goal should be to make your second personal sale. These are the most important short-term goals for you to accomplish. These two sales represent the foundation of your entire Enagic® business. In order to move up the distributor ranking system, making these two personal sales is a requirement. Your first goal: make two personal sales. Once these two sales have been made, each distributor can now really start to focus on what is necessary in order to move closer to the direction of their ultimate, long-term goal.

Not too long ago I realized something that had eluded me for nearly 4 years in this business. What I realized was that the goals that I had established for myself when I first started my business were completely wrong. I realized that my focus was completely in the wrong direction and that my business today has suffered as a result.

When I first started this business I was presented with the goal of becoming a 6A. I think the majority of people have it set in their minds that the first, and most important initial goal, is reaching the distributor ranking of 6A. Don't get me wrong, the ranking of 6A is a milestone position and one that any person should be proud of achieving. However, for the sake of building this business, setting your first major goal at becoming a 6A is really misdirected.

It was not until reaching the distributor ranking of 6A4-2 that I even realized I had done anything wrong; that my goal of achieving a personal ranking of 6A had negatively affected the long-term development of my business. Once I had a better understanding of the way the ranking system worked, I was able to recognize why this was a mistake.

You see, your first goal in this business should be created around the overall principals and ideas of the company and Mr. Ohshiro. The main ideas of the company are sharing, compassion and helping others. I knew this, and I try to practice this, yet, when I set out to achieve my first real goal, it went against everything the company stands for.

Instead of creating a goal based on the concept of sharing, the idea of being compassionate, with the intention of helping others, what I did was set a goal that was completely selfish; essentially making it all about me. Unfortunately, this is exactly what I ended up doing when I established my goal to become a 6A. As a result of my example, I taught my own distributors to do the same thing. And it was not until four years later that I realized that by doing this I actually hurt my business instead of helping it. Obviously this wasn't my intention, I just did not understand enough about the ideology of the company or the structure of the distributor ranking system to realize why my goal of achieving 6A was flawed.

Now that I have a much better understanding of the ranking system and, more importantly, the ranking advancement system, I understand where I really made my mistakes. Instead of making my goal be focused on me, my goal should have been about helping my distributors. If I would have set a goal to reach 6A2 instead of just 6A, my focus would have been on helping two of my distributors become 6A, which then would have made me a 6A2. By making my goal be about them, and helping them achieve their ranking, instead of making my goal be about me, and me achieving my ranking, I would've created growth in my business that would've been much more advantageous to me both short and long term.

If I could have taught my first distributors to have their goal be reaching 6A2, they too would have created a model where their focus was on helping two other distributors become 6A, not just helping themselves hit 6A. If you were to follow and teach this method, you would develop a sales organization positioned perfectly to maximize the distributor-advancement structure created by the company. This would also allow you to maximize the bonuses that are available when you advance in your distributor ranking.

As a result of what I have discovered, I am now recommending to all my new distributors that the distributor-ranking goal that they set should be that of 6A2. I am also recommending that, as they bring new

NOTES:

distributors into their own business, that they advise all of their new distributors to also set a goal of achieving 6A2. No longer will a new distributor have to set his or her goal to 6A. When you set your goal to 6A2, the sales volume that you need to become a 6A happens automatically once you have helped two of your personally referred distributors become 5As. All you would need at that point is one personal sale to make your 6A ranking official.

I don't want to make the idea of the goal of 6A2 to be really complicated, but I do think I need to explain it a little more so you will really understand the importance. Making this your goal and teaching your new distributors to have it be their goal creates an organizational development structure that allows for the most efficient use of sales volume as it pertains to distributor ranking and advancement.

When you first start this business the distributor ranking system can be confusing, which is the reason that understanding the need for the 6A2 goal may not make a lot of sense. In order for it to make sense, you really have to understand the way that each ranking of the distributors below you can trigger your own advancement.

Let's start by defining some of the basics of the ranking system. Hitting 6A means that you have at least 101 sales, with a minimum of three of those sales being personally sold by you, within the eight points of your sales group's organizational structure. It does not matter where the sales come from, as long as they are within your eight points, also known as "open volume". The fact that it does not matter where the sales come from in the structure of your organization is the reason that the goal of 6A can be problematic. You see, if these sales are spread all throughout your organization, then achieving the distributor ranking of 6A2 can become much more difficult.

A distributor advances to the rank of 6A2 once two of his or her personally referred distributors achieve the distributor ranking of 6A. By making your goal to help two of your distributors become 6A, you end up with the concentration of sales directly connected to those two distributors. This concentration of sales is what creates the structure that will move you into the higher distributor rankings more quickly.

It is much easier to move up to the higher distributor rankings, like 6A2-2, if you have developed concentrated growth within your sales organization. The "dash two" of 6A2-2 means that two personally referred distributors have achieved the distributor ranking of 6A2. Becoming a 6A2-3, would mean that two of your distributors in separate lanes have achieved the distributor ranking of 6A2-2, which means they each had two personally referred distributors that became 6A2.

As you may have noticed, there's a pattern here, and the one consistent piece that affects everything is an individual reaching the distributor ranking of 6A2. It is for this reason that I am now recommending that new distributors set a personal goal to hit 6A2 before anything else. Milestone advancements, like hitting 6A, will come automatically if your actual goal is hitting 6A2.

I am hopeful that this explanation is making sense to you; the last thing I want to do is make this even more confusing. Dissecting the complete advancement structure in order to fully understand how the 6A2 goal works can be difficult. I am hoping that distributors do not try to over think this concept and that they

NOTES:

understand how this idea falls in line with the core principles of the company and Mr. Ohshiro.

Unfortunately, many distributors will want to waste time trying to figure out why this is recommended instead of simply taking the recommendation. I can assure you of this, the only reason that I am recommending this strategy when it comes to setting your initial goals is because it is the best way to maximize the distributor ranking system in this business.

Just like my motivation for writing this book, which is to help distributors be more successful with their business, this recommendation is made with the intention of helping your team become more successful, your efforts to become more fruitful and your business to become more profitable. So remember, your goal, and the goal that you want to promote to your new distributors, is becoming a 6A2. The easiest way to achieve this is to simply help two of your distributors become 6As. Make it about them and experience success through supporting their efforts.

Now that you have a better idea about goals and goal setting, take some time and set your own goals. Make sure that you write them down; remember that goals that are not written down are nothing but notions or ideas. A goal that is written down becomes a tangible thing, it now actually exists.

Identify your long-term goal and then create some short-term goals that will help you get there. Using your goals, create your personal action formula so that you will know what needs to be done. And one of the most important things to remember is that a goal is only a goal. It is a place that you would like to get to. If you do not hit your goal, it does not mean you stop.

NOTES:

I believe in setting lofty goals, something high but attainable. I looked back at some of my own personal goals and realized that I had missed my goal of earning $500,000 in 2009 by about half. Should I be disappointed? Would you have been disappointed? Think about it, I missed my goal by half? I should probably have just quit. I obviously wasn't doing something right! But wait, even though I did not hit my goal, I still made about a quarter of a million dollars in 2009. Should I have quit? Yeah right, I don't think so!

Just remember that by setting your goals high, even if you miss them, you can still be doing okay! Just be sure to set goals high, but not so high that they are unrealistic. And never set them so low that they do not create at least some level of challenge to achieve them. Remember, the journey is the most exciting part of reaching the goal!

Now get out there and set your own goals, and have a great time on the journey to your desired destination!

NOTES:

Effectively Sampling Kangen Water®

There are lots of different ways to sample the water to people, but what I will share with you is the process that has been most effective for our team members. Keep in mind, this is not the only way to do it, but it is a proven way. But before I get into this, let me clarify a very important point.

There are some distributors in this project that do not recommend sampling the water. In fact, they are very vocal about not sampling people the water. They say it is too much work and that they are able to sell machines without bothering with providing prospects with samples.

While this might work for a few distributors, we adhere to the strategy of providing samples to our prospects. Why? The easiest answer is because that is what the most successful people in the project are doing. It is also because the water is a much more powerful seller than any of us will ever be!

The other reason is that by practicing this method, you also teach it to your distributors, and they end up doing the same with theirs. Sharing the water is an easily duplicated method to introduce prospects to the water. When you have a method to introduce a product to the market that is simple and duplicatable, you greatly increase your chances for success!

If you want to try to become a super sales person, that is your prerogative. Instead, I recommend that you forego attempting to become the next Ralph Williams (he was a pretty famous old-school car salesman) and simply learn how to give away free water.

NOTES:

Now let's dive into the most effective ways to sample Kangen Water®. First, we should discuss the different grades / levels of alkaline drinking water and which is the best for people to start drinking. The Enagic® ionizers produce 3 grades of alkaline drinking water, 8.5 pH, 9.0 pH and 9.5 pH. When I was first introduced to the water I saw these numbers and had no idea what they meant or what the differences were. In fact, I was a little perplexed as to why the increments between each grade were so small.

I am sure that by now you know the differences between the levels, but for the sake of giving you your money's worth, I will explain it. You see, the pH scale actually starts in the middle, at the neutral point of 7.0 pH. From this point every time you go to the left, a lower number, the pH level is in the acidic range. When you go to the right, a higher number, the pH level is in the alkaline range.

Just like the Richter Scale, which measures earthquakes, the pH scale is based on logarithmic progression, which means each whole number increase or decrease represents a tenfold difference. Simply put, a pH level of 8 is not one times stronger than neutral, it is ten times stronger. So, an 8.5 pH is actually 50 times stronger than neutral.

The higher pH level, and subsequent stronger properties, can create a stronger, more intense detoxifying effect for people that are more acidic. People detox in different ways and the process can be uncomfortable. Starting a person at a lower pH level will usually make the detox effect more gradual, so many people always start their prospects at the 8.5 pH level and then gradually increase the level.

I personally started with the 9.5 pH level alkaline drinking water and, for the most part, this is the level I give my prospects during sampling. Unless a person is older or has some pretty serious health conditions, I start them at 9.5 pH. Not that I want them to experience a severe detox, but I want them to feel something. I want them to know that there is something different about this water. I always joke around when asked what level I start people on by saying, "I start people at 9.5 pH; I toss them in the deep end of the pool!" But then I follow that statement up with, "But like a good lifeguard, I closely monitor them for the first few days, to make sure the detox is not too much for them."

It is also very important to warn them of the detox, although be mindful not to scare them off with horror stories of the most intense reactions people have had. Just let them know the most common detox effects, which are a slight headache, stomach discomfort and sometimes diarrhea. Equally important to warning them about the detox is explaining how positive the detox effect is for their body.

NOTES:
_____
_____

Your prospects have to understand that if they experience a detox, they are actually expelling built up toxins from their body. That the headache is caused by toxins leaving the body; that the stomach discomfort is often times from built up excrement releasing from the intestines and that the diarrhea is from your body finally being able to evacuate junk that has been stagnating inside of you. Getting rid of these things is a great thing, so encourage people that are experiencing a detox to stick with it and power through it. Most of the time, the detox does not last longer than a day or two.

Another important point to consider is that the state that your body is in today has taken your lifetime to achieve. That means for the good or the bad! It has taken time to build up the problems most people are faced with today. The water is able to expedite the cleansing process, so it is going to be felt.

The more gradual the process, the less it will be noticed. The more rapid the process, the more it will be noticed. Remind people that they really want those built up toxins out of their system as soon as possible and that the minor discomfort they may experience during detox is a small price to pay for how much better they will feel afterwards!

Now let's talk about what type of containers you should be using when you are sampling. When I first started in this project there was no direction given in this area. As a result, I ended up going to water stores and paying retail prices for 2 and 3 gallon containers. This became very expensive and slowed the initial progress. Well, I have never been satisfied with slow progress, so I quickly figured out how to become more effective.

NOTES:

I found several wholesale bottle companies and began sampling our prospects for 1/3 the original cost. Needless to say, I was able to greatly increase my sampling efforts. Then I found even lower priced bottles and discovered ways to make sampling more beneficial for my prospects.

Today I use the "Water Is Life" high quality, 1.25 gallon reusable water bags I designed. These are easy to store and designed to help convey the message of the properties of the water. These are an effective way to sample water and they maintain the properties better than just about any other option. These are what I use and recommend. If you are interested in learning more about these reusable water bags, visit www.going6a.com.

Be very careful not to use containers that are too large. They can be very awkward and heavy. Using large containers also exposes the entire batch of water to elements that will quickly reduce the beneficial properties of the water.

Learn from the mistakes we made and use the recommended types of water containers. It will make the sampling period much more enjoyable and rewarding for your prospects!

NOTES:

Many new distributors ask how long they should give samples; unfortunately there is not a universal answer. Most of the time we offer to sample for 30 days, it is important to establish an ending to sampling so the prospect does not think it will continue forever. But the reality is that some people only need samples for a week, while other need it for several months. Ultimately it is your choice of the duration you sample a person.

There is a process to sampling that, when used correctly, can usually result in the sale of a machine. It starts with you finding someone that is willing to try the water. We have already discussed ways to get people to try the water, so let's just assume you have someone.

The first thing you have to understand is that you want the prospect to get use to drinking the water, so you want to make getting the water as easy for them as possible, at least at the beginning. I will explain the sampling process in stages.

Stage 1 – Bring them fresh water every 2 – 3 days. Make sure they have a fresh batch and that they never run out of water during the sampling period. It is a good idea to check in with a new prospect often during this stage of sampling. Check if they are having any detox and establish open communications. Remember that during Stage 1, the prospect is doing you a favor by trying the water.

NOTES:

Stage 2 – They call you for more water or they report benefits / improvements. When this happens, the relationship changes from them doing you a favor by trying the water; to you doing them a favor by providing them with the water. You still want to bring them the water, but now make it a little less convenient for them and have them meet you someplace to get the water.

Stage 3 – You are providing water for them and some of their contacts, which is called "anchoring". I will cover anchoring in more detail later in this section. You now make it a little less convenient for them to get the water by making them come to you for it.

Stage 4 – You start becoming unavailable for a few days in a row, allowing some of the improvements to revert back to their original condition. If you get to this stage, this is the one that usually prompts a person to ask how they can get their own machine!

This process can take anywhere from a couple of weeks to a couple of months, it all depends on the person.

One way to greatly increase your chances of getting a sale through sampling is by using a technique called "anchoring". My friend Daniel is the one that turned me on to this technique and he is, by far, the best I have ever seen at actually doing it. The concept is pretty simple; sample a few more people through the person you are already sampling.

Here is how it works. Let's say you are sampling John and you have brought him a couple of batches of water and he has reported that he has experienced some sort of benefit. The next time you bring John water you bring a few extra gallons. You tell him to share those

NOTES:
_____

extra gallons with some people that he knows and cares about, to see if they also experience any benefit.

Then when you bring the next batch, you bring even more extra gallons and encourage him to give even more people the water. Since John has experienced some sort of benefit, he will probably be willing to share the water with his friends and family. It is very important to remember that the more people you are sampling, the greater the chance for a sale. Let me explain what often happens if you anchor correctly.

John shares the water with a few friends and one of them ends up sharing the water with his mother. The mother ends up experiencing some sort of benefit and the next thing you know, she is asking her son how to get one of the machines. Her son goes to John and then John calls you.

You tell John that getting the mother a machine will be no problem, but that he will need to ask his friend if he wants to get credit for the sale. Now John speaks to his friend and asks if he is going to give the sale to him or if he wants to get credit for the sale. Suddenly the fear of loss kicks in and John's friend is faced with the decision to also buy a machine so he can get credit for his mother's sale. John is also faced with the same dilemma.

Often times this type of situation will create a string of sales, where there was originally just one. So now the one sale to the mother turns into 3 sales: mom, son and John! This is the power of anchoring!! Learn it and use it!! Master how to give away free water and teach your distributors how to do it and share, share, share!!!

NOTES:

The Marketplace – You Are an Innovator!

When I first started as a distributor I was unsure what stage of introduction the Enagic® products were in this marketplace. This is a very important question when deciding if you are going to conduct business with a technology based product. After a lot of in depth research I discovered that this project is perfectly positioned for awesome opportunity, which is why I connected to it. I will admit that some of this is pretty boring, business related stuff, but it is important to those of us that understand what is going on!

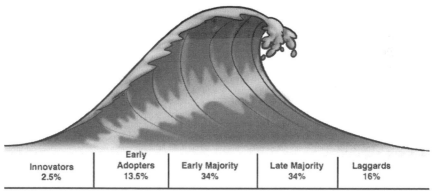

| Innovators 2.5% | Early Adopters 13.5% | Early Majority 34% | Late Majority 34% | Laggards 16% |

First off, you have to understand that technology products that succeed in this marketplace go through a very specific pattern of growth. It is a bell curve known as the "Diffusion of Innovation". As a technology product is introduced it goes through stages of marketplace penetration. Each stage represents a percentage of end users. Once a product enters into the "Early Majority" stage, it is almost guaranteed to succeed in the market. Products that do not make it that far usually fade away and are soon forgotten. There are several factors that will really determine if a technology product will become a consumer trend or if it will come to an abrupt end.

NOTES:

Before I continue, there is something that you have to understand. If you can somehow create a business connection with a technology product that is in the early stages of the marketplace introduction, and it becomes a major consumer trend, you can make an incredible amount of money during the process. But to spot a trend, you have to know what to look for, you have to know where it is in the marketplace introduction and you have to be able to do a little bit of forecasting, meaning that you have to make a guess about what will happen and then hope you are correct!

I believe that in order to truly appreciate what you are a part of, you have to really understand it, which is why I am including this section of the book. You see, a lot of what is in this section is information based on statistics and I don't think most people are familiar with them or how they relate to this business. I think that by explaining some of this, you will have a greater understanding of just how incredible this project really is!

To ride the wave of a consumer trend the first thing you have to know how to do is spot the trend. Thanks to our good friends the "Baby Boomers" this has been pretty easy for the past 50 years, as they have shaped the majority of the major trends. So, if you look at what their needs are in the immediate future, you can get a good idea of what trend is coming next. In the section "The Perfect Storm" I specifically address this aspect of the project, so I will not go into too much detail about how I concluded that this trend is coming right now. Let's just assume that it is. So, what's next?

The next thing is to understand the normal timeline for a technology product to be introduced into a marketplace. Typically technology products run on a 15 to 20 year

NOTES:

cycle, meaning that it takes this long for the product to initially enter a market and reach the plateau, which is when over 50% of consumers utilize the technology. The timeline and percentages of growth are usually not equal; in fact, it usually takes 7 – 10 years of initial marketplace introduction to get beyond the "Innovator" and "Early Adopter" stages.

If a product makes it past these two stages then there is usually a huge spike in end users. This is when a windfall of earnings can happen. At this stage a massive amount of consumers, roughly 35% of them, end up getting the product, usually in about a 3 – 5 year time frame. This is fast and explosive growth.

Now let's address the question you are probably asking: what's the real significance of this information and how does it apply to me? First, let's look at where we are in the trend cycle. This technology was introduced into this marketplace by Enagic® in 2003. It moved very slowly through the first stage of the trend for the first 3 years and then broke out a bit.

Officially, based on the actual number of units sold compared to the number of consumers in this market, we are still in the early "Innovator" stage. However, there is a slight difference with this particular technology when it comes to the trend cycle. You see, the technology has already been successfully introduced in another consumer marketplace, the Japanese market. While it is true that not all products that thrive in a foreign market will do well here, this product will do great. Why? Because it addresses a universal concern on this planet: health.

Here are some numbers to really think about. In Japan, this type of technology is in approximately 1 out of 6

NOTES:

homes. In the U.S. the ratio is about 1 out of 18,000. That means that for every 100,000 consumers in this market, there are only about 5 machines. Imagine the fortunes that will be made as this market grows to the size of the Japanese market!

Now I am telling you this for two reasons. First, so you understand the incredible potential of this project and so you will better appreciate just how massive this can become. The second reason is so that you will understand where the project is and what you may be faced with as you share this information with people.

Based on the numbers, we are still in the "Innovator" stage. Statistically this means that only 2.5 people out of every 100 that hear about this product should be ready to actually own it. The incredible part, and one of the most exciting aspects of this project, is that the actual percentage of people that end up purchasing a machine is much, much greater!

Again, during the first stage of the normal progression of a technology product being introduced is that only a few people out of every 100 are even willing to consider using and purchasing the product. The reality for us is that we are in the "Innovator" stage, with "Early / Late Majority" percentages. This is unheard of!!!

I had a distributor call me asking for some advice. She was a bit frustrated that more of the people she was telling about the water had not purchased a machine yet. I asked her how many people had she actually talked to about the water and the project and she told me she had just started about 4 weeks earlier and that she had only spoken to 6 or 7 people. She also mentioned that she had never done any kind of sales before and was not sure if she was doing things

NOTES:

correctly. I asked how many of the people she had spoken to were sampling the water and she said 5, which floored me! But the answer to my next question floored me even more! I asked if anyone was showing signs of buying and she said two people had already bought a machine from her!!!

Okay, maybe you don't fully understand the magnitude of this scenario, but I do! Let's break down the numbers and see what was really going on for her. First, she was successful in getting 5 out of 7 people to try the water, which represents roughly 70% of the people she had approached. That, by itself, is absolutely incredible. But then, 2 out of the 5 people she had sampled actually bought. That is a 40% buy rate, which is insane!!

In the world of sales, at this stage of the product introduction, the buy rate percentage should not be higher that 2% or 3%, yet this unskilled, novice to the project, was able to secure a 40% buy rate percentage. Not because of her expertise as a sales person, but because of the power of the water. This is why the percentages are so out of whack! Obviously not everyone will have the same results as her; some will have better, some will have worse. The important piece Is that these percentages are even able to be had! This is why I believe the project is about to explode.

You see, as more distributors join the business, more people hear about the product and begin trying the water. Why is the project still in the "Innovator" stage, because their simply are not enough distributors! This is why, as a distributor, you will want to add as many active distributors to your team as possible. The growth rate is about to become unprecedented and you can either benefit from it or watch it happen!!

While it is true the project holds incredible potential, the lesson I am trying to teach you with her story is that you should not get discouraged if everyone you talk to about the water is not receptive, they're actually not supposed to be! Remember, the statistics say that for every 100 people you talk to only 2 or 3 should be responsive. So, if you have spoken to less than 50 people and any of them have really listened, or agreed to try the water or have even bought a machine, you should say "WOW!!!", because you are way ahead of where you should be!!

Targeted Markets

It is important that you discover the "tools of the trade" in our business. While it is true that these include things like brochures, DVD's, audio CD's, etc., your most useful tool will be YOU and your experience!

The majority of the marketing efforts when you first get started in this project are normally directed towards residential consumers, but there are some nearly untapped markets just waiting for you once you have a solid knowledge base and once you have honed your skills of explaining the water. These are the commercial markets, which are expected to become very lucrative as more distributors gain the experience level necessary to approach them.

It is important that I warn against rushing into these markets prematurely, because if you do, you will most likely kill the opportunity of ever securing a sale or distributor. You see, unlike a personal contact, with a commercial contact, you typically DO NOT get a second

NOTES:

chance. You should really know your stuff before you attempt to tackle a commercial prospect.

Your experience with introducing the water to your hot and warm personal contacts is what helps you refine and hone your "pitch", which is nothing more than an explanation of the benefits of the water. The trainings you attend are the gateways to the information you will need in order to effectively work a commercial prospect, which is why it is so important to attend as many trainings as possible.

You have to remember that a commercial prospect will have much higher expectations of you, because they will see you as another sales person, trying to sell them something. When this is the case, you have to be able to not only explain the water, but also how it will benefit THEM, both personally and professionally. Just a quick side note, it is ALWAYS easier to get a machine into a commercial location by first getting the decision maker on the water personally, meaning that the decision maker has tried the water and experienced benefit. Most people are more inclined to integrate the water into the business side of their life if they have already decided to make it part of their personal life.

When dealing with a commercial prospect you need to know the fundamentals of the water, but also the specific benefits that it can create for their particular business. You also need to be able to answer any questions they might throw at you. This is why it is CRITICAL, PARAMOUNT, ESSENTIAL, and every other capitalized word that is synonymous with the word IMPORTANT, that you not attempt a commercial prospect prematurely.

NOTES:

How will you know if it is premature? If you have to ask yourself if it is premature...IT IS!!! You will know when you are ready. When explaining the water becomes second nature to you; when you do not have to turn to someone else to answer questions; when you are confident in your knowledge of the water; when you understand how the water can positively impact different commercial establishments, that is when you are ready. And when that happens...YOU WILL KNOW IT!

So now that we have established the fact that you need to be prepared for a commercial prospect, let's take a look at a few commercial applications that you might want to start with once you are ready. In this section we will look at restaurants, beauty salons, pets & vets and gyms.

Restaurants

Restaurants may be one of the easiest commercial markets to approach for several reasons. First, the water has numerous different applications in a restaurant environment; from use in cooking, for cleaning, for sterilizing and, of course, for drinking. Second, restaurants are one of the few commercial markets where you not only know them, but that they may actually know you, which, of course, can be to your advantage.

Just a quick side note, smaller restaurants are the best ones to approach, as larger, corporate restaurants, may be difficult to introduce the water. Most of the larger restaurant chains have the majority of their decisions made directly from the corporate H.Q., so trying to introduce the water to an individual restaurant in the chain may be very difficult. And trying to introduce the water to an entire chain...let's put it this way, I have already warned you against the perils of "Whale Hunting" and trying to land a large restaurant chain would definitely be a whale hunt! It is better to focus on the smaller "Mom & Pop" type establishments, where the decision maker is easier to access and where a buying decision can be made without needing the approval of committees and boards.

There are a few excellent resources that have been created to help approaching a restaurant much easier. Be sure that you have the necessary materials to present to a restaurant owner before you even make an appointment to sit down with them. Not having the correct support materials is like not knowing enough about the product...it can be a death sentence to the possible sale!

Most people have a favorite restaurant or two, where they have dined frequently enough to get to know some of the employees, from wait staff to the actual owners. If you have been doing things correctly, you may have already indirectly introduced these people to the water by bringing in your own bottle and by asking for an empty glass when they ask what you would like to drink (remember Drink, Drink, Drink!!?). Well, the relationship you have developed with these people is your ticket to take the next step with them regarding the water.
The fact that you know them and that they know you actually puts them into that "Warm Market" category, which should make gaining access to the right person much easier. But because this is a commercial prospect it is better to wait on introducing the water until you have gained the extremely important and necessary experience that we have already discussed. The only real exception to this is if the restaurant is owned by either a relative or very close friend, but even then you

NOTES:
_____

should initially introduce them to the water on a personal level, NOT through their restaurant.

Let's start by looking at the different grades of water and how they can be used in a restaurant. But before we do, I think it is important to determine which machines would be appropriate for commercial application. There are really only two choices of machines that can handle to demands of commercial use, which are the SD501 and the Super 501. While the other Enagic® models are great for consumer use, only these two machines have the needed power to tackle the commercial market.

Now let's get back to the different types of water. We will begin with the most obvious, which is drinking water. The restaurant can serve any grade of alkaline water, 8.5 pH – 9.5 pH, or they may choose to serve the clean water. What they decide to do is up to them.

By serving the alkaline water they create the opportunity to introduce the water to their patrons, which may end up leading to future machines sales. If they are not concerned with making future machine sales and don't want to worry about educating their staff or patrons about the alkaline water, they can simply serve the clean water, which will give diners a crisp, clean, great tasting glass of water with their meal.

There may actually be a benefit to serving the alkaline water, beyond the aspects of good health. You see, unlike filtered, bottled or even straight tap water, the alkaline water is micro-clustered. Micro-clustering allows for better absorption by the body, which means that if a person is drinking regular water with their meal, that water is taking up physical space in the stomach and is absorbing into their system slowly. We have all

NOTES:

experienced that "bloated" feeling from beverages. This feeling may very well lead to the diner feeling full, which may cut their dining experience short. The faster absorption of the alkaline water may help to reduce the bloated feeling, allowing the diner to enjoy their meal and maybe even have room for dessert, which will create a higher bill and more profit for the restaurant.

If they do decide to serve the alkaline water, it is a great idea to educate the wait staff to be able to answer basic questions. The owner should also offer to allow the wait staff to take water home with them. If they end up with positive benefits they may just end up purchasing a machine, which, again, would create additional money for the restaurant owner.

It is also a good idea to make the alkaline water a BIG deal if it is going to be offered to patrons. Beautiful bottles have been designed as a turnkey solution for restaurants that want to serve the alkaline water. They are available in different styles, with several different cap and printing colors to choose from. These are screen printed with Kangen Water®, with a decorative logo, along with an interesting description of the water on the back of the bottle. They can even be customized to reflect the restaurant name. If you have not seen one of these bottles, talk to your referrer or visit kangentoolbox.com to see images. If you are going to approach restaurants having one or two of these bottles as samples to show the owner is strongly suggested! Showing someone how good something will look always beats telling them about it!

There is another important point of consideration about serving the alkaline water, or even the clean water. Offering this water means that the restaurant is replacing some other water that was being served. In

NOTES:

some cases they are replacing straight tap water. I have actually spoken with several restaurant owners who have told me they have had many customers complain about the taste of the water they serve, so replacing their water with our delicious tasting water was a no brainer.

But then I spoke with a few restaurant owners who offered bottled waters for sale. What I discovered was pretty interesting. While it is true that the bottled water created a new profit center for them, in most cases the upfront expense of stocking an inventory of bottled water, and the storage space required, made it almost not worth it to them.

By adding Kangen Water® to their offering, they were able to completely eliminate the need for buying and storing bottled water, thus eliminating a major headache, extra expense and the continued active participation in the environmental nightmare created by offering plastic bottles of water.

There is one more thing regarding alkaline drinking water that I need to mention. As an independent distributor for Enagic® we are NOT allowed to sell the water that the machine produces. According to Section 14 of the Enagic Policies and Procedures Manual, sale of any water produced by an Enagic® ionizer can be grounds for termination of a distributorship.

That being said, if a person or entity IS NOT a distributor, they can charge for providing the water to people. So, what does this mean when speaking to a restaurant owner? What it means is that there is a way that a restaurant owner can be both a distributor and an end user, which would be the most advantageous scenario for them.

NOTES:

We already discussed the importance of getting a person personally committed to the water before they get professionally committed, so it would stand to reason that they will need two separate machines, one to handle the personal needs, the other to handle their professional needs.

The next aspect of the 8.5 pH – 9.5 pH alkaline water that you need to understand is how it can be used in the restaurant's kitchen. In my previous professional experience I actually dabbled in the kitchen of several restaurants. As a matter of fact, I came very close to pursuing a career in the culinary arts, as I absolutely love cooking. Unfortunately, like many things that we decide to try to transition from passion to work, the appeal quickly faded and I went in a different direction after about 3 years in the restaurant industry. But my time there has given me valuable insight to the inner workings of a commercial kitchen and how the water can be effectively used.

Before I continue, I would like to explain some realities of a commercial kitchen, just in case you have never had experience working in one. When you are in a SERIOUS kitchen, time and quality are the two most important ingredients. You have to get things prepared fast and they have to taste amazing! Anything that can improve either of these two components is something that a good chef will always be seeking! What we have just happens to help with both!

Let's start with time. Blanching, steaming, poaching, simmering, boiling...all of these are cooking techniques that involve heating water. One of the interesting byproducts of micro-clustering is the ability of our water to heat faster. I know it sounds ridiculous, because Kangen Water® conducts heat better it will actually come to a boil faster than regular water. As a result, this increase helps shave off a few more moments which help the food go from kitchen...to plate...to the customer more rapidly.

Now let's consider the effect the water has on taste, which is really the most important aspect of food served in a restaurant. Because of the absorption and ability to penetrate more effectively alkaline water is able to draw out natural flavors of both veggies and meats when they are cooked. The taste of soups, stews, sauces, actually any dish that is water based, is enhanced by the natural flavors that are drawn from the ingredients. Seasonings also become more robust and flavorful when used in alkaline water. Because more flavors are being drawn from the same amount of seasoning, less is needed to be used. In some cases the seasonings that are used are very expensive. When less seasoning can be used, without compromising the finished product, the restaurant is able to dish out great food, while saving money.

For a complete list and detailed explanation of all the different ways you can use alkaline water in cooking refer to *The Advantages Of Using Electrolytic Water* catalog that was included in the packet of information that came with your machine. All of the different ways listed in the catalog are excellent selling points to a chef that takes pride in the food they serve. You might want to get extra copies of this catalog to give to restaurant owners when you talk to them about the water.

Next we will cover a few of the ways that the Beauty Water, which has a pH value of 4.0 pH − 6.5 pH and is considered acidic, can be used in a kitchen. No it is not used to enhance the appearance of the food...it does not

NOTES:

make it more beautiful! However what the acidic water can do is pretty amazing.

The acidic water is excellent for cooking thin pasta. It will bring the pasta to an "al dente" consistency, which refers to the desired texture of cooked pasta in Italian cooking. It literally means "to the tooth". It also helps keep the pasta from sticking together during cooking. Acidic water is also excellent when used in batter for fried foods. Fried foods will turn out nice and crispy and will remain that way, not oily, even if they are left to sit for an extended period of time. It is also great for boiling eggs. Egg shells come off more easily and if an egg cracks during boiling, the yolk will not leak out of the shell into the water.

Again, for a complete list and detailed explanation of all the different ways you can use acidic water in cooking refer to *The Advantages Of Using Electrolytic Water* catalog.

Now let's talk about the Strong Kangen Water®, which has a pH of 11.0 or higher. If you have seen a live product demonstration or watched a video demo, then you have probably seen the residue that the Strong Kangen Water® takes off of tomatoes. Not only does this make the fruit or vegetable taste better, it also makes it last much longer. If fruits and vegetables are not being lost to spoilage as rapidly, then the restaurant is not spending as much money on fresh produce, which, again, helps to reduce cost and makes the R.O.I. (return on investment) of every plate of food higher! This means the restaurant makes and keeps more money!!
While the water is excellent to clean fresh fruits and veggies, it is also strong enough to be used as a degreaser in the kitchen. Let me tell you this, a

NOTES:

commercial kitchen gets dirty...FAST!! It is important that any spills or splatters are cleaned quickly, to help avoid any cross contamination or the possibility of food borne illness...the dreaded food poisoning. While it is vital to continuously clean the kitchen, no serious chef would ever let his kitchen be cleaned with chemical cleaners during food preparation. This, obviously, creates quite a challenge for those responsible for keeping the kitchen tidy while maintaining the integrity of a chef's kitchen.

The beauty of the Strong Kangen Water® is that it is water. If some of this water gets on food, it will not kill anyone, heck it won't even hurt anyone. Yet it will out clean almost every chemical cleaner out there. This is a HUGE selling point for a chef. Keeping chemicals out of the kitchen is something that almost every chef would love to do and the Strong Kangen Water® allows them to reduce a large amount of chemical cleaners.

Unfortunately the Strong Kangen Water® is only able to eliminate the need for some of the chemical degreasers that are typically used in a commercial kitchen; it does not have the power to replace all of the chemical cleaners, like the ones used for sterilization. However, we have water which can handle this job as well!! This takes us to the Strong Acidic Water, which has a pH of 2.7 or lower.

This is another one of the waters that really distinguishes our products from the competition. This water has been laboratory tested and shown to have the ability to effectively kill 99.999% of the germs present after only 30 seconds of exposure. Now I am not saying any 2.7 pH or lower water was able to do this, it was two Enagic® Super501s that were tested and it was the

NOTES:

water that they produced that was able to yield these results.

The results of these tests can be found in *The Secret Sauce* brochure, a great brochure that was created for the restaurant industry. It is this sanitizing power that will attract the attention of restaurant owners. Once again, they will be able to use water to protect against germs that may lead to food borne illness.

This grade water, along with the other grades, can all be used to improve a restaurant kitchen and the food that is prepared. One of the biggest advantages to a restaurant owner is the reduction of expense created by using cleaners, degreasers and sanitizing solutions / chemicals that have to be replaced after use.

Our technology literally provides the "factory" that produces all of these waters. And they can make it on an ongoing basis from the purchase of the machine. Hypothetically let's say that a restaurant is spending $100.00 every month for their cleaning supplies. Now just so you understand, this is a very conservative number, as there are numerous cleaners that are used in a restaurant.

Being fair, let's say that the machine is only able to eliminate 75% of the cleaners that the restaurant uses, which means that they are able to save $75 per month on the cleaning supply expense. It has been established that an Enagic® water ionizer can last as much as 20+ years, if maintained correctly, but, again, let's be fair and reduce that number by half. That would mean that the 10 year savings to the restaurant owner from just the cleaners that they are no longer using, based on the numbers in this example, would be $9000.00.

NOTES:

Even if the total 10 year cost of owning a machine were $7000.00 - $8000.00, which would include the cost of the machine, the replacement filters, cost for cleaning, etc., the owner would still end up saving money by adding the machine to their restaurant.

This also does not take into account any additional money that may be made by offering the water as a premium beverage, the savings created from using less spices and beverage ingredients like coffee and tea, the savings created from reducing the amount of spoilage of fresh produce and even the additional revenue that can be created should a customer from the restaurant decide to purchase a machine. Obviously, adding this technology to a restaurant has the potential to be very beneficial!

There is one more aspect of the machines that can create an even bigger advantage for a restaurant, which is using it to provide water samples for prospects. We refer to this as being a "Water Hub". Here is what happens if a restaurant decides to become a water hub. The restaurant opens their doors to allow anyone to come to the restaurant to get free samples of the alkaline drinking water.

This means that they make it available for their own patrons that might want to try the water, as well as other distributors that may have prospects in their area. It is important to mention that if a prospect from another distributor were to decide to buy a machine after sampling the water, the sale would go to the other distributor, not the restaurant. You might be asking yourself, why would the restaurant want to do give away free water to help someone else make a sale?

NOTES:

Here is how it is beneficial to the restaurant. When you open your doors as a water hub, you are able to decide when and how people can get water. Let's say that from Monday – Friday a restaurant has 2 slower times, from 10:00 am – 11:30 am and from 2:00 pm – 4:00 pm. If they decide to be a water hub, they can say, water is available only Monday – Friday, during those specific hours. And they can limit the amount of water to 1 or 2 gallons per visit.

Now, the restaurant is creating new foot traffic during the times that were slower for them. While these people are coming to the restaurant to get water, they still gotta eat!! This is an excellent opportunity for the restaurant to convert someone getting a water sample into a paying customer. Some restaurants offer a special diners discount for their "Kangen Friends", which has helped increase the revenue of the restaurant.

All in all the integration of an Enagic® water ionizer into a restaurant has the potential to create incredible benefit for the restaurant, the patrons and any local distributors / prospects. Knowing these benefits can help you introduce the water and close a sale to the restaurant, so be sure to review this section several times and get proficient with the information!

There have been some new tools and resources introduced that make approaching restaurants even easier for distributors. There is a commercial markets video training, available for those wanting to learn more about the best way to approach a restaurant.

Beauty Salons / Spas

One of the waters that the Enagic® water ionizers makes is actually called "Beauty Water" so it only makes sense

NOTES:

that the water would be a great addition to a beauty salon! One important point to mention is that a healthy, beautiful exterior starts with a healthy, beautiful interior.

Any salon that decides to implement the technology into their establishment should encourage their clients to drink the water, which will create a solid foundation on which to build their exterior beauty! We will start this section discussing a few of the ways that the Beauty Water, which has a pH value of 4.0 pH – 6.5 pH and is considered acidic, can be used in a beauty salon or spa. This grade of water is great for both skin and hair care.

Beauty Water is excellent for washing the face. The astringent properties of the acidic water are very effective in toning and firming the skin. It can be sprayed on or patted onto the skin using a washcloth.

The Beauty Water is also great for the hair. When used as a rinse after shampooing it helps reduce tangles and brings out a radiant shine and luster.

For a complete list and detailed explanation of all the different ways you can use acidic water in for skin and hair care refer to *The Advantages Of Using Electrolytic Water* catalog.

Next let's look at the Strong Acidic Water, which has a pH of 2.7 or lower. We have already discussed the sanitizing power of this water, so let's consider how this could be used in a salon / spa.

Most full-service salons offer some sort of nail care and, in addition to manicures, many offer pedicures, which often includes a foot soak to soften the cuticles of the toenails. Ironically, most of the spread of bacteria in

NOTES:

salons comes from the very foot soak that is supposed to help prepare for the pedicure.

When a salon gets very busy, as many of them often do, many times the foot bath basin that is used to soak the feet is not thoroughly cleaned, which can lead to a buildup of bacteria.

In recent years it has been discovered that a pedicure infection caused by exposure to these bacteria can become a very serious thing and that any unusual symptom noticed immediately after a pedicure should not be taken lightly. Many people have had amputations and even died as a result of infections contracted while receiving pedicures. Yes, it's that serious!

Although pedicures can be very beneficial to the feet, contracting an infection while getting one can be very detrimental to a person's health. If the pedicure tools used are not properly disinfected, most notably the bath basins used to soak the feet, bacteria can be allowed to build to dangerously high levels.

The bad part is that any break in the skin can allow harmful bacteria get into the bloodstream. It could be a scrape from scratching a bump too hard, a nick from shaving or even an insect bite. All of these can lead to a pedicure infection by allowing germs to enter your body.

It is very possible also, to contract bacteria that are resistant to antibiotics. The usual kind of bacterium associated with pedicures that is resistant to antibiotics is MSRA or Methicillin-Resistant Staphylococcus Aureus. This strain of staph bacterium is resistant to all of the penicillin and as a result is extremely difficult to treat.

NOTES:

If this strain is contracted, the infected area may have to be amputated in order to save the rest of the body from an untreatable infection. If left to progress and spread too long, it will most likely lead to death.

While this may seem like an unlikely possibility, it happens more than people would ever imagine, which is why this is PERFECT for us!! You see, MSRA was one of the bacteria that was tested and was killed in the laboratory tests.

So imagine that the foot bath basin in a salon is not only cleaned with the Strong Acidic Water after every use, but that the actual water used to soak the feet is 2.7 pH Strong Acidic Water!

This would allow the cuticles to soften, it would help kill any bacteria that may have been on the foot prior to going into the water and it would help ensure that bacteria never even gets a chance to start forming, let alone getting to dangerous levels that could potentially kill someone! What a huge selling point this would be for any salon that offered pedicures!

The Strong Acidic Water could also be used to help sterilize combs and brushes, as well as counter tops, salon chairs, floors and any other surfaces that may come into contact with clients more frequently.

For a complete list and detailed explanation of all the different ways you can use Strong Acidic Water refer to *The Advantages Of Using Electrolytic Water* catalog.

These are the two main waters that most salons would use directly, but, just like the restaurants, they could also open their doors as a water hub and create more

NOTES:

foot traffic. This could, of course, lead to new clients and more business.

If you decide to approach a beauty salon or spa it is important not to forget the Anespa DX. This is an awesome product for locations offering any sort of mineral bath or mineral bath treatment. The water produced from the Anespa DX is great for the skin and hair and leaves a person feeling refreshed and rejuvenated.

Always keep in mind that with a machine in a business location, all of the employees would also have access to the water. They would be able to take it home and share it with their friends and family. This may, and often does, lead to sales, which would be an additional revenue stream for the salon.

There is a brochure that has been created to approach salons and spas. It specifically addresses the needs of a salon and how an Enagic® water ionizer can help meet those needs. Be sure to have some of these before you ever go to the salon.

There are many other uses for the different grades of water in a salon, but for the sake of this section we will keep it to what has been covered. If you decide to approach a salon, think about a few other ways that the water could be used. Go and visit a few different salons and really watch what they do and how they do it. This will normally lead to the discovery of a few more ways that the waters can be put to good use!!

Pets & Vets

Leona Helmsley, a hotel and real estate billionaire, became known as a symbol of 1980's greed and earned the nickname "the Queen of Mean" after her 1988 indictment and subsequent conviction for tax evasion. She passed away in 2007. Her estate is estimated to be worth billions, yet she excluded two of her four grandchildren from her will. While the people in her life did not seem to make much of an impact on her, the same cannot be said for her dog, Trouble. In her will she left her beloved white Maltese a $12 million trust fund.

Then there was a high-stakes game of "fetch" for the multimillion-dollar estate of a Florida woman that pitted her only living child against a tiny Chihuahua named Conchita. Heiress Gail Posner lavished the beloved pooch with a $3 million trust fund, along with the run of the $8.3 million Miami Beach mansion she inhabited. To her son she left $1 million.

These are just a couple of examples of how much a pet can mean to a person. It actually speaks volumes to the fact that some people will spend more money on their pets than they would on themselves. This is what makes the potential of this targeted market particularly interesting.

The pets and vets market actually includes a wide variety of different businesses. You could approach someone that provides dog walking services to a small animal hospital, and everything in between! Veterinary clinics, animal trainers, pet hotels, pet stores, equestrian centers, pretty much anywhere that the business is in some way, shape or form concerning pets or animal care.

For the most part, you would take the same approach of sampling the water to a person when dealing with a pet related business. Allowing an animal owner to have

NOTES:

samples of the water for their pet to try is usually the most effective way. Simply provide water that they give their animal and let the water do what it will.

It is important that you realize that an animal lover is going to know their animal. They will be able to recognize if their dog suddenly has more energy. My own dog is a prime example.

When we got our machine I immediately started giving our dog 9.5 pH alkaline drinking water. Within just a few days I noticed a major change in his overall energy level and his mannerisms. Before the water he used to have a slight limp on his back right leg. After the water the limp seemed to vanish. How? I have no idea, other than maybe my dog, just like us, was dehydrated, which was affecting his muscles and joints.

The thing that really struck a chord with me was that our dog, that was starting to show visible signs of age, seemed to be acting younger and more energetic every day. This may sound funny to someone that does not own a pet, but he seemed happier. And the only thing I could attribute to the changes was the water, as I had not changed ANYTHING else!

Another interesting point about animals is that they CANNOT be victims of a placebo effect, which means if they start acting different or showing signs of improvement, it's not just in their head!! IT is actually coming for something...namely the positive benefit being created by drinking the water.

When sampling a pet owner it is important that you provide water for the pet AND the owner!! Your efforts will be much more effective if they both see some benefit, but that will only happen if they both are

NOTES:

drinking the water. Many people ask what pH level to start a pet. Because most pets do not live a "stressful" life, meaning no job to worry about, no screaming kids to get to school, no deadline that they have to meet, it is probably best to keep the pH level at 8.5. Remember, the pH level is all about balance, so it will probably take far less to get a pet balanced, as it would a human. The 8.5 pH is the best bet for pets.

The 5.5 pH Beauty Water is great for hair and skin, so using it on an animals coat will bring out a shine and a luster that will make them look great.

One more very important thing to consider is the time of year when sampling a pet. If it is summer, they will probably need more water, since most pets are outdoors, at least for part of the day, and they consume more water during hotter days. Just make sure they have enough to make the sampling effective!

Gyms & Sports Clubs

Let me start by saying that after reading this section you should NOT plan to run down to your local 24-Hour Fitness and try to sell them an ionizer! This section will focus on smaller, independent gyms and sports facilities. Remember...NO WHALE HUNTING!!!!

A gym is probably one of the most appropriate places to have an Enagic® water ionizer! Think about the clients that use a gym and what they are doing while they are there. First, these are people that care enough about their health to intentionally travel out of their comfort zone in the pursuit of fitness and they pay money each month for the privilege to do so! Then they push themselves to the brink of exhaustion and then push a

NOTES:

little more. They end their workouts dripping with sweat. So, what do they need now?

They need to re-hydrate!!! And not with Gatorade or Powerade or some processed sugar filled flavored beverage or an overly acidic bottled water...they NEED to replenish their body with ionized alkaline water...they need KANGEN WATER®!!!

It is important that I mention a few things before you consider approaching a gym with the water. First is that you really need to know your stuff if you are going to talk to the owner of a gym. This person has decided to make a career out of providing health and fitness to their clients, so they will have very high expectations when it comes to someone trying to introduce something into their business model. Just make sure that you really know the how's and why's of the water before ever attempting to approach a gym!

The basic principles of the water still apply here, with the different levels of alkaline drinking water being the same as in the other targeted markets we have discussed. But there are a few things that I can share with you that are excellent points if you were to have the opportunity to speak with the owner of a gym.

Let's start with a buzz word that everyone is familiar with, which are antioxidants. Most of us have heard of antioxidants, but few people actually know what they are. They just know they are supposed to be good for us. We will begin with a review of antioxidants. I covered them in the *Learning the Lingo* section, but I think they are important enough to cover on more time.

These are substances or nutrients in foods and beverages, having a negative oxidation reduction

NOTES:

potential, which can prevent or slow oxidative damage to our body. Oxidation, which is a regular function of metabolism and cell function, strips an electron from certain molecules.

These molecules, called free radicals, must then steal an electron from a nearby molecule to repair themselves; which means that the nearby molecule must now steal an electron from another molecule and so on and so on. This vicious oxidation cycle ends when an electron is taken from a molecule which has an excess electron available to donate.

Antioxidants act as "free radical scavengers" by donating the excess electron to the free radical, which quells their hyper-reactivity and renders them harmless. Many of the serious health problems facing American's today are attributed to oxidative damage. Antioxidants may also act as powerful immune defense enhancers, which may reduce the risk of disease. Alkaline water is a very effective natural antioxidant because of its very high negative oxidation reduction potential.

Because Kangen Water® contains large quantities of negatively charged ions that act as antioxidants it provldes the body with an abundance of free radical fighting ammunition and helps promote cellular health. Promoting health on a cellular level will obviously be good for anyone dedicated to health and fitness!

The next important aspect for you to know is regarding weight loss. Let's be real, one of the main reasons a person goes to a gym is to lose a few pounds. Well, drinking the water can actually assist in the weight loss process.

NOTES:

Most people do not realize this, but water is a natural appetite suppressant. A lack of water in your body can lead to over eating. The brain does not differentiate between hunger and thirst. So, many times when you think you are hungry your body may actually be sending signals to let you know it is thirsty. Ever eat and eat and eat, but still feel hungry? It's because what your body is wanting is water...not food, but we have lost the ability to recognize the difference ourselves.

In addition to being an appetite suppressant, water also serves several other key roles that can affect weight loss. Water assists in the digestion, absorption and assimilation of food. If you are not drinking enough water you won't get the full benefit of the nutrients in the food you eat.

Water also assists in the excretion of waste from the colon and kidneys. If you don't drink enough water you can get constipated from a buildup of unreleased toxic fecal matter that adheres to the walls of the colon and you can put excessive stress on your kidneys.

You have to realize that the human body is made up of 60 -70% water, so staying hydrated is important if you want to stay healthy...the two go hand in hand! Consider the fact that the blood is over 90% water. The blood is the body's transport system, spreading nutrients and bringing oxygen throughout the body. If your body is dehydrated, then the blood will be thicker and the flow of blood though the body will be reduced. This reduction can have very harmful results!

The last couple of paragraphs were more about general health and water, so let's get back to the specific topic of weight loss. A balanced metabolic process in the body can have a major impact on weight loss. There are

NOTES:

trillions of cells in the human body; these have an acidic interior and the exterior interstitial fluid that surrounds the cell is alkaline. Without proper balance between the interior and exterior of these cells, the cells have a difficult time flowing into surrounding tissues. This results in the body's metabolism being very low, which, can lead to weight gain.

Kangen Water® has an alkaline pH level that can help balance your body's acidic environment. Being in balance leads to higher metabolism, and with higher metabolism, it is easier to lose the fatty deposits that have gathered as a result of buildup of acidic waste in the body. Bottom line...weight loss and increased energy are easier to achieve when the body is properly hydrated!

Now let's take a look at how hydration helps with overall health as it pertains to fitness and exercise. There is no question that, next to the air we breathe, there is nothing more important to life than water. As we have already stated, water helps the body absorb and digest nutrients, while eliminating toxins. Water lubricates our joints; helps protect our tissues and give flexibility to our muscles, tendons, cartilage and bones. Each cell in our body contains water!

We need to be sure to consume sufficient amounts of the right kind of water, and evidence is mounting that water with a higher pH level and high levels of negative ORP is the right water! People have been experiencing more stamina, less fatigue, quicker recovery time, better cellular hydration, greater flushing of toxins and an overall improvement of the body's ability to perform at peak efficiency.

NOTES:

- 135 -

As you may be realizing, there is a lot to this, should you decide to approach a business like a gym. But, be assured that introducing the water to a gym is NOT an experiment. It has been done and has been very successful. A very prestigious gym in Brentwood, CA, called Joe's Gym, was one of the first to recognize the potential of the water for their clients.

The owner, Joe Mancuso, took proactive steps to make the water available to his staff, clients and trainers. He removed the gyms regular drinking fountains and created Hydration Stations, complete with an SD501, cups, brochures and literature and even a flat panel TV that played a DVD that explained the properties of the water and why they should be drinking it.

I had the honor of sitting down with Mr. Mancuso when I recorded the audio CD, *Most People Think All Water Is the Same*, along with Wade Lightheart. Both gentlemen were a wealth of knowledge about the interaction between the water and the human body, but it was something that Joe said about implementing the water in his gym that really stood out to me.

"When you operate one of the most prestigious private gyms on the west side of Los Angeles, you need to always be providing your clientele with the very best trainers, state of the art equipment and the latest information about health and wellness. From the moment we installed an Enagic® SD501, our members have been drinking this amazing water when they work out and then refilling their bottles to take more water home with them. Many have reported faster recovery times from injuries, more stamina, they're sleeping better and some have even commented on improvements in the appearance of their skin. We brought the machine in as an experiment, with its overwhelming acceptance, there's no way we can ever see removing it."

If you decide to approach a gym, or any other business, it is vital to your success that you be PREPARED!! Be educated; have the correct materials and information; research the business and come in with a solid understanding of how the water can help THEM.

Selling to commercial accounts can make you a lot of money, but you have to know what you are doing. If this section has taught you anything, I hope it has taught you that professional level preparation is the most important tool you can have when trying to land a commercial account!

NOTES:

The Medical Industry – Thrive or Alive?

Now that we have discussed where the project is in its marketplace introduction, I would like to address a couple of areas that may create "speed bumps" in your journey as a successful Enagic® Independent Distributor. The first is the medical industry. While you would think that the medical community would be flocking to find out more about how the water works and how it may help their patients, in general, they do not.

I think it is important that you understand why this is the case, mainly so you don't waste a lot of time trying to convert everyone you know in the medical industry to a new way of thinking. Before I dive into this section, let me clarify a few very important points. The people that I am referring to, as being less than receptive, are in what would be considered the traditional "Western Medicine"

field. The old, diagnose based on symptoms and then prescribe medications accordingly. What we have found is that the majority of these types of people are very set in their ways and become very defensive of their methodologies when something as basic as water is introduced as a possible way to improve overall health.

But then there is a subset of the medical industry that is made up of people taking a natural or holistic approach to health and wellness. These people are usually very receptive to new ideas and most of them are more than willing to try the water and consider the possibilities.

The reason I am addressing this subject is because I get, on average, 1 or 2 calls every week from someone asking why their medical doctor is not showing interest in the possible benefits of the water. While this is not always the case, it is what happens more often than not. Since this book was written to help you overcome obstacles and to understand this business, I felt that getting to the root of this issue was very important!

To have a better understanding of why, let's take a look at the medical industry as a whole. Again, as I have said numerous times throughout this book, the following is MY opinion on this topic and is not necessarily the opinion of the company or anyone else. I think to understand the current state of the medical industry; you have to understand how it started.

I am part American Indian and I think the foundations of tribal life are an excellent place to begin. You see, in tribal days there were a couple of people in the tribe that held positions of authority and importance. The most obvious would be the Chief, the person responsible for the tribe. But the person that came in a close second to

NOTES:

overall importance was the Medicine Man. While it was the duty of the Chief to provide leadership and direction to the tribe, the job of the Medicine Man was to keep the entire tribe healthy.

It is true that being Medicine Man would bring with a certain level of respect and authority, but I think there is a much more important reason why being a successful Medicine Man would be very important. Was it because of the bigger teepee in the most prime spot of the village? Was it because of the faster, flashier horse he got to ride? Or was it because he actually had a personal, vested interest in the health and wellbeing of every member of the tribe?

I believe that the last option makes the most sense. You see, while the members of the tribe were dependent on the Medicine Man to help them stay healthy, the Medicine Man was dependent on the rest of the tribe for his own needs, so if they were in poor health, it would directly affect him. If the Chief were sick, the tribe would be without necessary leadership; if the warriors were ill, the tribe would be without protection; if the hunters were not healthy, the tribe would be without food; if the squaws were sick, there would be no clothes.

In the tribal world, every one of these things would have impacted the Medicine Man directly, so his wellbeing was directly connected to that of the tribe.

Now, let's look at the modern medical industry. Right off the bat, the fact that it is referred to as an "Industry" is a very bad sign. When medicine became an industry, then it became a business, which means it centers on profit. I believe that it was the introduction of medical insurance back in the 1950's that really created the

NOTES:

current "Medical Industry". It changed the dynamic of medicine being a "calling" into being a "profession".

Believe it or not, there was actually a time when a person would attend medical school because they really wanted to help people. Nowadays, why do most parents want their kids to become doctors? Because of the PAY!! Not because it is a noble thing to do. It's because it is a way to make good money and lead a better life style.

Not so long ago, medicine in this country was more like the tribal model than the current model. There was a doctor that would service the needs of people in their own community. You remember, the days of the "house call". Much like the Medicine Man, these community doctors relied on people around them for their own wellbeing. Then communities grew and hospitals were joined by clinics. Then health insurance started limiting which doctors a person could see and patients went from being a familiar face to a number. The doctor's personal vested interest in the health of each patient has vanished!

Patients have become customers. In business, what are the best kinds of customers? Repeat customers! So, is the medical industry of today really geared towards wanting to keep their customers healthy? Or is it more suited to keeping people just healthy enough to be able to go to work to earn the money needed to cover their co-pay?

Ask yourself this question: does it seem like the medical industry wants people to thrive or just be alive?

The answer to this question speaks volumes as to why people in this industry are less than receptive to

NOTES:

something that might actually improve the long term health of a person. There is a lot of money in people being, and staying, sick and the reality is that getting and keeping people truly healthy is not financially prudent for the medical industry.

There is another powerful force that greatly influences the medical industry, which are pharmaceutical companies. I know, for a fact, that doctors are encouraged to recommend or prescribe specific brands of medications and that a lot of money is spent by pharmaceutical companies to help ensure that their brand is the one being prescribed.

In the paragraph above I said "I know, for a fact...", let me explain how I know. A few years back, before I ever knew about Kangen Water® and the benefits of drinking alkaline water, my wife, Susan, worked in the back office of a medical doctor's private practice. It was her very first day on the job when I learned the lengths that pharmaceutical sales reps would go to in order to have their brands be the ones recommended.

When Susan got home from her first day we sat down and she told me all about it. She told me about some of her co-workers, what her basic duties were, some of the more interesting patients and, finally, she told me what a great lunch she had and that she did not even have to leave the office to get it.

She went on to explain that one of the pharmaceutical sales reps had stopped by the office and dropped off lunch for the entire office. I thought that she had lucked out by having her first day coincide with the day lunch was provided for the whole office.

NOTES:

The next day I found out that the lunch had been much more than coincidence. When Susan got home after her second day we chatted again about how things had gone and she, again, ended by telling me that lunch had been provided for the entire office, only this time by a sales representative from a different pharmaceutical company.

By the end of her first week the office had been provided with lunches for the entire staff every single day; each day by a different rep from a different company! And these were not quick, fast-food type lunches. These were full meals from restaurants like California Pizza Kitchen, Pat & Oscars and even P.F. Chang's. It got to the point that Susan completely stopped making any plans for lunch, as food ended up being provided for the entire office every day that she worked there.

I did not realize it at the time, but this ended up giving me some pretty clear insight to just how influential the pharmaceutical companies were becoming when it came to the way doctors were "treating" patients. Just like doctors, prescription drug companies were looking for life long customers, not just temporary users and they would do what they could to jockey into the best position possible.

Now I am sure if any of these representatives were ever asked directly if they ever did anything to try to influence a doctor's decision to recommend their drug, they would say "NO!" or "Of Course Not!". They would probably contend that any recommendation of their brand by a doctor was strictly based on the effectiveness of the medication.

Just so you don't think my viewpoint about this topic is founded solely on biased opinion, please allow me to

NOTES:

share with you portions of an article written by Ransdell Pierson and Bill Berkrot, published by Reuters on March 31, 2010. This article is being referenced strictly for educational purposes.

Pfizer paid $35 mln to doctors over 6 months

Pfizer Inc on Wednesday said it paid $35 million to some 4,500 doctors and researchers from July through December 2009 for a variety of services, including speaking fees, expert advice and work on clinical trials of its medicines.

The world's largest drugmaker last year agreed to pay a record $2.3 billion fine and plead guilty to a criminal charge related to improper promotions of 13 of its medicines, but said the new disclosures were already in the works before that widely publicized settlement...

...About $15.3 million, or some 44 percent of Pfizer's reported payments over the last six months of 2009, went to about 250 research organizations for clinical trials that began after July 1, or for payments made between July 1 and December 31 for clinical studies.

Some 1,500 healthcare professionals were paid an average $5,000 each for expert advice, while 2,800 doctors were paid an average of $3,400 in speaking fees to lecture peers about Pfizer's drugs, the company said. The most highly compensated doctor received about $150,000 during the period, Pfizer said...

...Other large drugmakers, including Eli Lilly and Co, have recently begun publishing payments to doctors on their websites. But Neese said its disclosures go beyond those recently established by other companies, in that they include payments for clinical trial research, Neese said.

Pfizer said its payment disclosures will become more detailed a year from now, under a corporate integrity agreement with

NOTES:

federal health authorities related to the drugmaker's $2.3 billion fine and settlement last summer...

...Pfizer in September was slapped with the huge fine by the U.S. government after being deemed a repeat offender in pitching its now-withdrawn Bextra arthritis drug and another dozen medicines to patients and doctors for unapproved uses.

Pfizer pleaded guilty in 2004 to an earlier criminal charge of improper sales tactics and its practices have been under U.S. supervision since then.

Speaking engagements, in which doctors are paid by drugmakers to discuss their medicines with groups of other physicians, have been among the most controversial industry marketing practices.

By law, companies are forbidden to promote their drugs for uses not cleared by the U.S. Food and Drug Administration. But some companies allegedly have greatly boosted prescriptions for their drugs by allowing or encouraging paid speakers to discuss such "off-label" use of their products...

So, as I am sharing this information with you what am I really trying to say? What is the point? To me, the bottom line is that medicine is a business and businesses try to make money. The reality is that if your business is to treat sick people, you will not be successful if you make everyone healthy!

If you can wrap your head around this concept, then it may be easier for you to understand why the medical industry is not eagerly reviewing information about the water.

It also lets you know that, as we try to educate average, everyday people to the benefits of Kangen Water®, there is an entire industry working hard and spending a lot of

NOTES:

money to convince these same people that what they need is what they have to offer!

There is one more thing I would like to share with you, which is the medical industry in Japan. I did a lot of research on this topic and found that, by law, all hospitals in Japan must be run as non-profit. For profit companies are not allowed to own or operate a hospital. Japanese people live longer than anyone else on Earth, think about that!

NOTES:

The Beverage Industry – "Zombie Drinks"

In the previous section we covered the medical industry and why some of those affiliated with it may not be willing to consider trying the water. Now, we will cover some of the obstacles being created by the beverage industry.

The very first thing I need to make clear is that the bottled beverage industry is HUGE and there is a lot of money involved. The industry also is more far reaching than just the liquid in a bottle or can. There are so many different facets of it that it is easy to see why the major players in this industry are so powerful. The U.S. bottled beverage industry has been around since 1835, when the first soda water was bottled for sale. Since then the industry has grown considerably and stretches globally. For the sake of this section, I am going to

NOTES:

concentrate on two main aspects of the U.S. bottled beverage industry: water & soda. The reason I think it is important to discuss the bottled beverage industry is because they spend an incredible amount of money each year to get consumers to buy their products. They do it through slick marketing campaigns, celebrity endorsements and a variety of other extremely effective methods. It is important that you consider these efforts as you are making your way as an Enagic® Independent Distributor because their efforts are influencing the decisions of the people you are talking to about Kangen Water®. Many of these companies have been very successful in creating brand loyalty and some drinks have become a part of people's daily routines.

Not only are we trying to get people to try our water, in some cases we are asking them to stop doing what they normally do. We try to educate people to some of the hazards of different bottled beverages and these same people can become defensive, because we are challenging what they believe and what they do. This is one of the reasons it is very important to really understand the industry, so you know what you are up against. The bottled beverage industry spends tens of millions of dollars every year in market research, marketing and advertising. Their ultimate goal is to not only make their beverage a choice of the consumer, but to make it the ONLY choice of the consumer. They strive to create both brand recognition and brand loyalty.

Knowing that this is something you will be going up against is extremely important! It will allow you to develop an approach that will not make a person defensive. Remember, what we tell people about our water may be interpreted as a challenge to what that person has been doing, in some cases, for their entire

NOTES:

life. People don't want to be told that the decisions they have made were bad ones, it makes them feel stupid. So be very careful not to end up coming off as a "know it all" and insulting their previous life style choices.

I believe the truth about many bottled drinks will come out and consumers will be more aware of the possible health risks associated with the consumption of these products. But, just like smoking, I think that there will be plenty of people that will disregard the consequences and will continue to pop the top and keep on drinking. In order to effectively share information with the people you speak to about our water and about bottled beverages, there are a few things that you should know.

First, we know that the vast majority of bottled waters and soda have a pH value that makes them acidic and, most of them, have an ORP value that make them an oxidant, which is, of course, bad for the body. Second, we know that there has been a tremendous increase in life style related diseases, especially in children. In fact, the #1 killer of children 14 and under in America is cancer. This is where we have to use a bit of common sense and deductive reasoning in order to make sense of this increase. Fortunately, the increase has actually happened within a period of time that we can actually see the progression! We can pin point when the increases started, which can then let us figure out what life style changes were happening at the same time.

The increase in childhood disease is noticeable about 25 to 30 years ago. Now some will contend that the increase is due to better detection and increased awareness. Unfortunately, this argument is completely unfounded, as the medical community has had all of the necessary testing equipment to discover these conditions for decades. Since we can determine when

NOTES:

the increase started, let's consider what changes were happening in America 25 to 30 years ago. Probably the biggest change was the significant increase in production of and consumption of processed foods and fast foods. Another major change was the introduction of soda as a regularly consumed beverage. For those that are a bit younger, this statement about soda may not make much sense, as we all know that soda in America has been around for well over 50 years. The difference in the past 25 – 30 years is the way soda was being consumed. You see, back in the olden days, soda was considered more of a treat than an everyday beverage. It was something that was available when children had behaved. It was a luxury that was only available every so often.

It was the combining of a fast food meal with a soda based beverage that really introduced soda as more of an everyday product, which, again, can be pinpointed to about the mid 1970's as the time when this trend started to sweep across America. In the mid 1980's the trend for bottled waters started to hit, beginning with more affluent people drinking carbonated artisan waters like Pierre in upscale restaurants. Drinking bottled water started as more of a status symbol than anything else, but it spawned the trend that has now made the bottled water industry one of the biggest industries in America. If these bottled beverages were not unhealthy, then this would be a trend that would fine. However, we now know that nearly all of the bottled beverages consumed in the United States pose some sort of possible health issue for the consumer.

With the ingredients in modern day soda it is easy to understand why they might not be very good for us. Heck, some of the listed ingredients read like a chemistry experiment. Even sodas that claim to be

NOTES:

"natural" have preservatives, flavoring and artificial coloring. Unfortunately, the bottled waters out there are not much better. One of the reasons that bottled water ends up being acidic is because of processing requirements. In order for water to be bottled it is supposed to either be heated to a boiling point, to kill any potentially hazardous contents, or go through a reverse osmosis / distillation process, which will render the water void of any contaminants. Actually, it renders it void of anything! Once the water goes through one of these processes it becomes acidic. Even if minerals are added to the water after processing, which most big bottlers do, the water still remains acidic. Unfortunately, most consumers have no idea that the beverages they know and love may actually be bad for them. I believe, and again this is MY opinion, that within the next decade enough information about the negative effects of some of these bottled beverages will be discovered and that, following suit with the Surgeon General warning on cigarettes, that there will be an actual warning cautioning consumers to the potential harmful effects of consuming the product.

Then, of course, there is the aspect of the environmental impact created by the bottled water industry. Back in the 1950's the bottles were primarily made from glass. Today, the vast majority of the bottled beverage industry uses plastic bottles. While these bottles are recyclable, the reality is that only about 27% of plastic bottles are actually recycled. This means that over 70% end up in landfills, highways, waterways, parks and many end up in the ocean.

NOTES:

While there is plenty more that we could discuss regarding the bottled water industry, I think that this is enough to give you a foundation of basic information. Obviously, if you want to find out more there are resources everywhere! One of the best is the Internet. If you want to expand your knowledge about the bottled beverage industry, just do some searches on "soda", "bottled water" and "plastic bottles". Just these three key words / phrases could keep you busy for days learning all sorts of things about the industry!

NOTES:

Building Value – Eliminate the Issue of Cost

One of the biggest issues facing distributors is the aspect of the cost of the machine. You have to understand that if you are going to tell someone the cost before you give them any background of the product or give them a chance to experience what a difference the water can make in their life, all you're doing is giving them a 4,000 dollar question mark. When this happens, prospects don't have anything to base a value on, so all they see is the price. A price that, at this point, has absolutely no justification in the mind of the prospect.

This is why we recommend that you give the water for people to try before discussing any cost or business aspects. You do this because that's where the interest is found. You have to realize that for a person to purchase any type of high ticket item they need to understand the benefit of the product. If at all possible, they will want to see results before they make a financial commitment. What it will eventually boil down to is the need to feel that this machine will create at least 4,000 dollars' worth of benefit or value to the consumer. The reality is that only the consumer can come to that conclusion and we have found that sampling the water is the easiest way to allow them to decide.

We sample the water because when people feel better they recognize value in the machine. Consider this, if someone were to come to you with a magic pill and they told you that it would make you feel wonderful and everything they said was true and they asked you how much you would pay for it, the answer would, of course, vary, depending on who was being asked. An older person who may have lost some of their good health would probably put much more value in that magic pill

NOTES:

than a healthy young person. People value things that make them feel better and it really helps if they can personally experience some kind of benefit before they have to make a purchase. People need to know that a product actually works before they can really determine the value of the product. By experiencing benefits created by the product, they begin to understand how valuable the product may be to them.

You have to realize that the product itself has no value. If you take away electricity and a water source, all you end up with is an expensive paper weight! It is the byproduct, the water, that establishes the value of the machine and we are able to give the byproduct away to let people see if the water creates any benefit for them. This is why we sample the water and let people put value on the product themselves without trying to push the product onto people. The way that a lot of people make it big in this business starts with them seeing a change in themselves, and then deciding if the product has value in their life, and then they develop the desire to share the same type of changes in the lives of those around them. The best salespeople in this product are the ones that sampled the water, reaped the benefits, purchased a machine and then let those around them reap the same benefits by letting them sample the water.

Make sure that you are building value for people by sampling the water and letting the consumers see what a difference the water can make in their life, without trying to sell them anything or pressure them into anything. This is a different sales process than just about anything out there; it actually makes the water the "sales person". The water can sell itself better than you or I ever can, because only the water can provide the benefit a person needs to recognize its value. Remember the old saying: "seeing is believing!"

NOTES:

The 60 Second Internet Expert

Let me start by telling you that sometime during your experience as an Enagic® Independent Distributor you WILL run into a person that has become an overnight "expert" on ionizers after spending a few short minutes on the Internet! You have been warned!! Now, let's talk about the best way to deal with this or, better yet, never have it happen in the first place.

There are a few realities that we have to deal with as a direct distributor. One is that people, especially people you know pretty well, have some deep seeded issue with a person they know making money from something they purchase. It seems like they are fine with some celebrity being paid millions of dollars to endorse a product, but share some of those marketing and advertising dollars with someone they know and suddenly there is a conspiracy to defraud them! I am not sure why, but some people get really weird about it.

NOTES:

Believe it or not some people act like there is an award for disproving the information you share with them and they want to be the one that gets the award!! But knowing that this is the case is what allows us to prepare for it!

When you first talk to someone about Kangen Water® they get exposed to a new list of words and terms that I like to call "keywords". They hear new things like "Enagic®", "Kangen", "ionizer" and "alkaline"; with just those few words a person can go to a search engine on the Internet and find a whole slew of negative information about the product. This negative information has been posted by competitors and is the main way that they sell their products.

These other ionizer companies have become experts in using the Internet to create the look of a major company, even though we have discovered that some of the "Corporate Headquarters" are nothing more than a private residence in the middle of nowhere! One very important thing to remember is that the majority of "competitors" that are advertising on the Internet are not the actual manufacturer of their products. They are simply distributors trying to sell inventory and, as such, have very little to lose by providing false or misleading information. They have even gone as far as purchasing "search engine keywords" so that when a person types in the word "Enagic®" in a search engine, an advertisement for the competitors product appears at the top of the page.

Now you might think, "That was pretty clever!" Well clever is not the right word, the right word would be illegal! You see, "Enagic®" is a registered trademark name, which is owned by Enagic U.S.A. So is "Kangen Water®". Yet both of these terms are used by

NOTES:

competitors to divert consumers away for helpful information and towards their inferior products. See, this practice just goes to show you that some of the competitors will go to any lengths, including violating Trademark Infringement laws, in order to sell their product. Ask yourself, is that the kind of company you would want to do business with? Instead of using all the trickery and foolishness on the Internet I have always asked, "Why don't they just let people try their water instead?" But I am getting off topic, so let me get back to dealing with our 60 second experts.

When a prospect is left to do their own "research", here is what ends up happening. First, the people you talk to will get the basic information from you and then will go online to look for a way to disprove everything you told them. Again, I don't know why they do this, but they do! They will put in some of the keywords I mentioned into a search engine and then find the smear campaigns initiated by the competition.

They will then read just enough to feel they have sufficient ammunition to tell you that you were wrong and then they contact you and tell you about all the negative information that they found about your project. The real reason this happens is not because these other websites are so convincing and accurate, but because you haven't given you're prospect enough information to let them know what they are going to find when they do their "research". Come to grips with the fact that they are going to go online and do some kind of search. Don't just close your eyes and hope that they won't...they WILL!! Since you already know that they are going to do it and since you already know what information they will find; introduce them to it before the Internet does, it has a much different affect if you do.

Let them know about the good, the bad, and the ugly that they will find online. Step one is to inoculate them by letting them know what they will run into. You see, if you don't include this information when you are talking to your prospect, when they find it on their own it makes them feel as if you were hiding something; which opens them up to believing the things that other people are posting online about the product.

Those things contradict everything you've already said; discrediting everything you've said. However, if you let them know what they are going to run into before they run into it, it shows that you know what you're talking about. It also shows that you are not afraid of the information that they will find, because you know the truth behind it. It verifies that you have taken the time to familiarize yourself with important information, which ends up strengthening your credibility and weakening the effectiveness of what they find online.

Here's what I'll typically do. I'll explain the basics of the water and then tell the person the following: "I expect you to do what every savvy consumer does, which is go home and go online and check out the information we've discussed. Since I know that's what you're going to do and, since I would expect you to do this, let me tell you some of the things you will run into, so they don't come as a shock to you."

Then I tell them exactly what they are going to find. "When you put in our company name in a search engine other companies will actually pop up. They've purchased keywords to make their products pop up when you search for our company. Then they will try to sell you on the price and not the quality of their products. Since I know you are a better consumer than

NOTES:

- 158 -

that, I know you won't pay attention to the hype, but I wanted to at least warn you about it."

"Heck, some of these other companies even have fake websites that look like a consumer reports review. Just so you know, there is not a single unbiased site you'll find online about water Ionlzers. If you want to know who is behind each review website, just check out the machine they rank as the best. That will be the company behind that particular website."

"Actually, most of the other companies compare their products to the products made by Enagic®, saying that they are the same, only cheaper. Now, as savvy consumers, we know when similar products are being compared, an inferior product is trying to be elevated to the level of a superior product. Just so you know, Enagic® doesn't compare themselves to anyone!"

When you are giving people this information, don't sound like you are trying to slam the competition. Instead, just be straight forward and direct. When they go online and find all the information you've warned them about, it makes you a credible source of information, because everything you said is exactly what they found. Simply warn your people about what they are going to run into. This simple warning can inoculate them from getting "infected" by the online garbage. Let them know what they will experience, by doing so you will be protecting them and you!

Don't think that by not telling them you are shielding them, because you're not. By not telling them you are only helping the competition make your prospect feel as if you were hiding negative information from them. If they feel like it's been hidden, they feel like it's been hidden because it's true. Forewarning them about what

NOTES:

they will find prepares them and reinforces what you have said as the truth. It says that what they find online has already been discovered and researched and proven to be false. This should help eliminate the creation of the dreaded 60 Second Internet Expert!

Choosing the Right Product for Your Customer

In this project there are two types of people that will purchase a machine, strictly users and people that want to work as Enagic® Distributors.

For people that are strictly users, the easiest way to determine which machine is best for them is by identifying how they will be using the machine. This is when your listening skills need to be in full force. Which machine will depend of several variables: is this person alone; do they have a family; how much water will they be making; what issues have made them want to drink the alkaline water; why are they wanting the machine and how will they use it?

A person that wants to work the business as a distributor really needs to have an SD501. This machine is best suited to handle the needs created by being a distributor. The SD501 has the plate size and power necessary to create properties strong enough to be able to sample the water, which is the most effective way to build an Enagic® distributorship. For distributors this is the absolute best machine because it produces the highest quality water to sample to people. There is no question about that.

When determining what product your customer needs, you need to ask them if they are interested in becoming a distributor. If they say yes, or even just maybe, then they really should be focused on the SD501 as the product they are going to purchase. If they have an objection to the price and want to go for the cheaper one, you should remind them that this machine is completely tax deductible and encourage them to check that out with their tax people. Also explain to them that because of the way the machine is going to be used

NOTES:

they need one that is strong enough to produce properties that will last long enough to sample and the challenge of ongoing constant usage. It's not to say that the other machines aren't able to be used in the same manner, but the SD501 is the best and produces the best outcome. Also, if your customer is going to work this as a business, they need to be willing to invest a little bit in their business and go for the product that will produce the best water to share with others. The bottom line is that each person interested in purchasing the machine is going to have some kind of usage planned for it. If the person is only interested in drinking the water and not using their machine for any other purpose, then all they really need is the alkaline drinking water, which means that a smaller machine would be perfect for them.

Knowing your product is an important part of helping your customers select the right one. For example, the LeveLuk R, which is the lowest priced ionizer that Enagic® offers, is a basic starter unit. It has the smallest plates and lowest power properties. As such, it will have the weakest properties of all the Enagic® products. It really should be a backup machine, not a primary machine. By allowing a customer to select this unit because of the lower price, you are really cheating them, because, ultimately, they will not get the quality of water and life out of the machine that they expect to.

Take everything that your customer is looking for into consideration to help them get a machine to fulfill their needs. It's easy to think that everyone needs the same machine, but it's not always the case. Make sure to address their needs before trying to decide what they should really get. If you're willing to listen your client will tell you exactly what they want and, more importantly, exactly what they need.

NOTES:

The Perfect Storm

In the year 2000 the motion picture *The Perfect Storm*, starring George Clooney and Mark Wahlberg, was released. This was the big screen adaptation of the real life events as they happened to the Andrea Gail, a small commercial fishing boat, in the North Atlantic in 1991. The boat and her crew became the victims of a weather convergence that had never occurred in recorded history. Two powerful weather fronts and a hurricane all came together at the exact same time to create what has been called "The Perfect Storm".

In my opinion, we are seeing another perfect storm brewing right in front of our eyes. The Perfect Storm of Opportunity! In the movie, the "perfect" storm came as a result of several smaller conditions coming together to create a great big one. Individually each was powerful, but they did not have the tremendous fury that was unleashed until they joined forces. This project sits on the brink of a similar convergence.

Instead of intense weather fronts moving across the ocean, we have marketplace conditions that have lined up to create what might be the most incredible opportunity we will see in our lifetime. This "Perfect Storm" has been building for decades and all of the most important components are coming together at exactly the right time, which puts you in exactly the right place to benefit from the windfall that is happening.

This storm consists of the following factors coming together: proven product; marketplace need; growing health issues; dissatisfaction with traditional medical care; environmental impact; lifestyle consequences and economic instability.

NOTES:

Proven Product: This product has been tested and perfected for over 35 years, yet practically no one in the U.S. has ever heard of it. The benefit has been proven in the Japanese market for decades. The technology is solid and the product is the best in the industry. The quality of the product is one of the biggest and most important pieces.

Marketplace Need: If you understand the driving force behind the U.S. retail market, then you will completely understand why the timing is perfect for this product. The Baby Boomers, people born in America that are between 50 – 70 years old, control the majority of the money in this market and move industries based on their wants and needs. Currently, their #1 need is good health. They are realizing that their lifestyle choices are having serious consequences and they are looking for ways to not only improve their overall health, but also to ensure a better quality of life. This is a massive group of individuals and they are all coming to this realization at the same time.

Growing Health Issues: Health concerns are at an all-time high!   Cancer has now become the #1 killer of Americans, overtaking heart disease. Even our children are being affected. Today, the #1 killer of children under the age of 14 is cancer. The World Health Organization (W.H.O.) expects cancer to become the #1 global killer within just a few short years. Numerous other health issues are also on the rise and people are looking for ways to improve and maintain their health.

Dissatisfaction With Traditional Medical Care: Many people in America are sick and tired of Western Medicine and pharmaceutical companies. People are realizing that the promise of a "quick fix" through the taking of prescription medications is actually no fix at all

NOTES:

- 164 -

and that, for all of our technology and medical advancements, in the area of health we are greatly lacking. People are dissatisfied! It is this dissatisfaction that is inspiring many people to seek out alternative health care and natural remedies. As a result of declining confidence in traditional medicine, many people are taking personal responsibility to educate their selves about health and are taking journeys of self-discovery about the simple steps to good health. They are also finding that the natural approach is actually leading to improved health and quality of life.

Environmental Impact: People are finally starting to realize just how much we are impacting our environment. They are realizing that what we are doing is not sustainable and that changes must be made. News organizations around the world have reported on the devastation that plastic water bottles are having on the environment. "Going Green" is becoming more important and suitable options will be needed around the globe.

Lifestyle Consequences: People are now realizing that lifestyle choices are a major contributing factor to overall health and wellness. They are discovering that things we once thought were good for us are actually very bad. They are finding out that what they are doing each and every day is actually contributing to their own failing health. This realization is prompting people to take a serious look at their own lifestyle choices and to make changes to create a better state of balance.

Economic Instability: The current state of the economy is actually a major benefit to this project. Many people have been displaced from their job or are in fear of losing their current employment. This is creating a whole new group of people that are willing to look at an

NOTES:

unconventional means of earning income, because the conventional means have completely let them down. These are people that may not have ever considered self-employment as a serious option, but now are very willing to not only consider it, but pursue it very aggressively.

Individually, none of these factors would be enough to sufficiently fuel the explosive growth of a retail product; but when combined, they create an environment of growth and potential that may just be bigger than anything anyone has ever seen in business.

Our "Perfect Storm" is one of opportunity and you have the chance to harness all the power that it has to offer. Be sure that you understand the immense power and potential of this project and that you relay this information to your business prospects. This is the type of scenario that seasoned business professionals look for, but seldom find, so be sure to share it with them. The stars have aligned; all the lights are green; you are truly in the right place, at the right time!

NOTES:

Play It Straight

If you are going to be successful in this, or any other project, it is important that you establish and maintain an excellent reputation. While this may sound easy enough, "Playing it straight" can be difficult because, unless you get caught, the only person you have to justify your actions to is yourself, and it can become very easy to justify questionable ethics once money becomes involved.

This section is geared to help you understand what temptations are out there and the best ways to stay away from them. It is also geared towards guiding you in a direction that will help you establish and maintain a stellar reputation.

The first thing you need to do when dealing with a prospect is be honest with yourself. Above all, be honest with yourself! While it is true that who a prospect decides to be sponsored by is entirely up to them, it is also true that if you are not the person that originally introduced them to Kangen Water®, you should seriously consider the consequences, should you decide to try to get them to sign under you.

Unfortunately, there are distributors in this project that will shamelessly swoop down on another distributor's prospect and will sign them up, without a second thought. This is one of the reasons that you should always "mind the store" when it comes to your prospects! Be there with them at meetings; personally get them water samples; work with them consistently; treat them like they might earn you a lot of money, because they just might!!

NOTES:

While most distributors choose not to go down this questionable path, there are those that do and you should be mindful of their existence. You should also strive to not end up labeled as one of them! Once you get labeled as a distributor that goes after other people's prospects, that label will stick with you, in this industry, forever!

Let me give you a perfect example of what I mean about playing it straight. The illustrator of this book, Nick Gonzales, was introduced to me by a fellow distributor, who is not in my organization. She told me about this young, talented artist that was very interested in the project. I met Nick, answered some of his questions about the product and business, spoke to his mother over the phone about the water and then ended up discussing having him do the illustrations for this book.

During the time that all this was happening, Nick did not yet have a machine, nor was he a distributor. Boy oh boy, was he ripe for the picking!! Here I was, with this energetic, enthusiastic young guy wanting to work the business as a distributor and I had already been established and introduced as a leader in the project. Without me even telling him, he knows that, if I wanted to, I could be of great assistance to him in developing his business. It would probably not be very difficult for me to convince him that I would make a great sponsor and that with me he could achieve success much faster and much bigger.

The only problem would be that he is not and was not my prospect!! He did not learn of the water or the business through any effort of mine. My answering his questions cannot justify me trying to take him from another distributor. Heck, it was my choice to answer his questions and my decision to be helpful. That, by no

NOTES:

means, would give me the right to think I should be able to sponsor him! I think that this is where distributors go astray. They think that if they answer a question or offer to help someone that they somehow become entitled to then be in the running to be the sponsor of that person. If your motivation for offering assistance is to try to steal a prospect from a fellow distributor, then don't offer to help. Don't do anyone any favors!!

The worst thing is that most of the distributors that choose to engage in this practice are really bad sponsors and, in most cases, will leave you and start looking for a new victim before the ink on the application is even dry.

The best rule of thumb is to look for and work with your own prospects. Don't go looking for people that have already been introduced to the project or that are actively working with another distributor to try to sway them to buy their machine from you.

In the case of Nick it was obvious to me that I had no right to discuss being his sponsor, so the topic never even came up. In fact, this section was completely written before I even told Nick that I was going to be using him as an example.

No matter how you try to justify it, if you are not the one that introduced someone to the project, then you should not be their sponsor. In fact, if you ever have to try to justify putting your name as the sponsor of a new distributor, then you probably should not be the sponsor!

The bottom line when it comes to sponsorship is playing it straight and things will work out much better, in both the short run and long run.

NOTES:

Setting the Foundation

When you start as an Enagic® Independent Distributor your initial efforts will basically be going to setting the foundation for the growth of your business and your future success. There are a couple different ways to do this.

You can do it very haphazardly and just rush through it and get it done quickly, without paying much attention to the skills of the distributors you've sponsored and if they're learning the processes to build their own business, which in turn would build yours. If you build in this way you will end up with a very unstable business. If you try to build a business with no foundation, it will end up collapsing.

I don't know if you've ever been by a high-rise construction site before and seen that before a big building goes up, there is a huge hole in the ground first. This is because the bigger the building, the higher it is going to go, the deeper the foundation needs to be to support growth and let it reach the heights that it is possible of reaching.

What you need to do is realize that your business is a lot like the construction of a high-rise. When you're setting the foundation at the beginning you might not be seeing a lot that looks like progress, but the deeper your foundation digs, the higher and more successful your business can grow.

You need to have the mindset of an architect. You need to solidify the foundation of your business so that it can grow to the heights you want it to grow. What I recommend to all my team members, especially in the beginning, is to put out as much effort as possible, dig

NOTES:

that hole! You are learning how to give out water; how to share information; how to get your new distributors trained; you are digging your foundation. During this time, you have to be patient. It may not look like you're making any progress, it may feel as if nothing is really happening, but it is, it is just below, out of sight.

The pillars of your foundation are the first few distributors that you sponsor. Make sure they are strong! You have to be sure that they are getting the right training. Take them to meetings with you, that way you'll both be the training you will need. Take them to events like executive luncheons; use every opportunity to get them trained properly and at the same time get yourself plenty of training. Doing these things help secure the foundation of your business.

It may seem as if you're not getting anywhere right off the bat, but if you understand what is happening, it will be okay. There are times when you're business can grow quickly, but even when it does most people are never satisfied with what they have or what they're getting. They always want more, like they could be getting more or deserve more. Don't fall into this trap. Be patient and have realistic expectations.

In this business you could quite literally cover all your initial costs and be in profit mode after just the first 30 to 60 days. Most small businesses take between $50,000 and $250,000 or more, just to get them started, and they usually fail within the first two to five years. It also typically takes two years or more before a business owner breaks even in their business, meaning they recoup their original investment and finally enter into profit mode.

NOTES:

Dig deep your first couple months and realize that you might not see big results immediately. Remember, this is a real business and can produce like a real business, if you treat it like a real business. So dig deep, secure your distributors, and make sure their foundations are secure, which will make your business stronger in the long run.

The Blind Leading the Blind

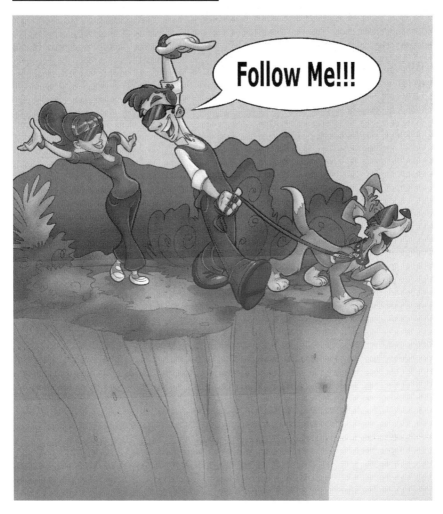

Throughout this book we will be discussing aspects of leadership, which is a very important part of this business. We will be discussing what it takes to become a leader, the responsibility that goes along with being a leader and how assuming a leadership role can greatly help as you build your business. But in this section I will be focusing on how a new distributor can

NOTES:

identify and connect with an established leader and why it is important to do so.

In this project the distributor ranking of "6A" has been used as a sort of merit badge of leadership, but I have to warn you that the title is not always an indication of a leader. In fact, the title is not necessarily even an indication of success in this business. Some 6A's might actually get mad at me for discussing this, but I think it is important for a new distributor to know the facts, so they don't end up being fooled into following advice that comes from nothing more than an empty title!

There are actually several different types of 6A's in this project. I will start by explaining each so it will be easier for you to identify the ones you will want to learn from.

First is the "Successful 6A". This is a 6A that knows they are successful, because their success shows itself every day. They are making personal sales, they are receiving daily overrides, they enjoy multiple bonuses, their sales group is properly built and productive, they provide support and are needed by their team, they have created many success stories and they are busy! The successful 6A is easy to spot and is the kind of distributor that you would want to be. They lead by example and it is an example worth following!

Then there is the "Mediocre 6A". This is a 6A that thinks they are successful or that tries to fool others into believing that they are. They are always waiting by the mailbox hoping for a check, they get small bonuses, if any at all, they seldom provide support because their team has stopped calling, they have very few success stories and the ones they do have happened by luck!

NOTES:

This is one of the 6A's you really have to watch out for and that you will want to distance yourself from! They love to get recognized as a 6A so they can offer up advice to those that will listen. Be cautious of this type of 6A and keep your distance. They might be nice enough people, but they really will not be able to help you in developing your business. Remember, true leadership stands out, so before you select a leader to work with, make sure they really are a leader and the type of distributor you would want to become.

The next type of 6A is the "Broke 6A". This is a 6A that knows they are not successful, but they like the attention and the recognition the 6A title gives them. This is a distributor that became 6A on a fluke or they were carried to 6A by a distributor in their team that became successful. They know there will be no checks in the mail, they know they built incorrectly or not at all, they are loaded with excuses and they blame their lack of success on everyone and everything else.

In my opinion, this is the most dangerous type of 6A. You see, the Broke 6A is a distributor that is often looking for the "B.B.D." (Bigger Better Deal) and may be willing to use their title to jump to another project and to try to take some of the newer, inexperienced distributors with them. When this happens, and unfortunately it does happen, they try to use their title of 6A as a sign of success and knowledge, implying that following them to a different business would be a smart move. Well, let me warn you right now, don't be fooled!!! Following a Broke 6A will probably lead you to the same level of success as them. You guessed it - - - BROKE!!

These are pretty much the different types of 6A's. There is one more, the "Invisible 6A", but as the name implies, you won't be seeing much of any of these, so they are

NOTES:
_____

really not even worth mentioning! Now that you know the different types of 6A's it should be much easier to identify the ones that are really leaders.

I guess it is time to discuss the actual title of this section, which is "The Blind Leading the Blind". You see, as a new distributor, you are kind of the second "Blind" in the title, meaning that you really do not know what you are doing. The worst thing that can happen to a new distributor is that they start getting help from someone that is just as blind as they are!! As a distributor it is your responsibility to find the best ways to help your business. One way to do this is to work with someone that has already achieved some degree of success in the business.

It is best to start with the person that sponsored you into the business, but they may be just as new as you. When this happens it is best to look to the distributors above you for guidance. The reason this is best is because the distributors above you benefit financially from your success, so it is in their best interest to help you.

As you start your search, be watching out for the fake leaders I talked about earlier. Try to find a person that you like and that likes you. What you are really looking for is a mentor or a coach. Someone that is willing to teach you the game and show you the ropes.

So what happens if you are unable to find a distributor above you that will work with you or that you want to work with? Then it is time to go outside of your team and see if one of the other leaders will work with you. Keep in mind that they are not obligated to do so and that if a leader from a different team decides to work with you it is probably because they like you and

NOTES:

genuinely want to help you succeed. If you get lucky enough to have a leader from a different team willing to work with you, you should make it your goal to become independent as quickly as possible. This will show that you respect the time of the leader and that you are really trying to maximize their willingness to   assist you.

Ultimately what you should be trying to achieve is becoming a leader yourself. You should strive to be a Successful 6A.   You should become the type of distributor that new distributors want to provide them with help. And when the time comes and you are asked for help from a new distributor, remember how it felt when you were in their shoes and step up to the plate and help them out. That's when your success becomes bigger than you and when what you have learned in this project really makes a difference!

And if you are unable to connect with a specific leader personally, understand that there are plenty of other ways to connect to them and to utilize their knowledge and experience. You can tap into their training events, conference calls, project presentations, executive luncheons, etc.   This is one more way you can use established leaders in this project to help build your business!

NOTES:

Developing Your Team

Going Wide vs. Going Deep

While building strategies can end up a hotly contested debate, I am going to cover this aspect of the project based on what I know works and based on what the Mr. Ohshiro, President & CEO of Enagic®, recommends.

Mr. Ohshiro recommends building your team by personally sponsoring as many distributors as possible. Then, provide the support necessary for them to become successful. This is the simplified explanation of the recommended building strategy.

NOTES:

While there are different mind sets out there on the best way to build, Mr. Ohshiro's strategy seems to be the one that creates the best results. But the debate will rage on regarding building wide or building deep, so I will address both.

If you are looking for daily checks, which means you go to your mailbox and get checks on a daily basis, you want to build wide. This means that you are constantly sharing water and working with new prospects. That you are continuing to develop new "legs" or "distribution channels" by sponsoring new distributors. This will create both commission and override checks.

If you want great incentive checks, make sure your organization develops depth, but do it the right way! Some people try to "create" depth by "placing" new distributors under an existing distributor in their team. While this may seem harmless, it usually does not accomplish what was intended and sets a very bad example.

Placement of a new distributor under an existing distributor is usually done to try to motivate the existing distributor, by helping them.

Unfortunately, what it usually does is make them an even less productive distributor. The person doing the placing has created a model of the existing distributor getting something for doing nothing. So why would that motivate them to do something? They just learned that doing nothing is what creates a reward for them, so then they start doing even less than nothing!

There is actually a story in the Bible that addresses this type of situation. The summary of the story is "Give a man a fish, you feed him for a day; teach a man to fish,

NOTES:

you feed him for life." Giving a fish to an existing distributor will not accomplish anything in the long run. In fact, it may actually help in crippling the distributor. Teaching your distributors how to fish will serve them for a lifetime. So become a teacher, not a giver!

Instead of trying to "create" fake depth by placing distributors, actually build it. How do you build depth? You support your sponsored distributors and teach them how to be successful. Then you make sure that they duplicate your efforts with their own distributors. This will create a solid leg that will eventually grow on its own. Each time a new distributor is added to the leg it is building depth for your organization!

As I have already stated, what you really want to try do is enjoy the best of both worlds by building a strong team sideways and then help support them so they build their own strong teams. Just remember, for daily pay build wide, for incentives build deep and for success, build both!

If you want to really insure the success of your business you have to be sure you're building the correct way. The best way to build is by learning how to master the basics and then do them consistently! Share the water; share the business & build for events!

One of the important things to remember is to treat this like a business, a real business, not as some kind of hobby. Treat it like a business and it will pay like a business; treat it like a hobby and, well, you get the idea! I have mentioned this before and I will mention it again, because it is important, your people will do what you do, not what you say to do, because that's what you're teaching them. Realize that you are setting the

NOTES:

example that they will copy. So set an example that will make you more money!

If you can learn to build wide and teach your people to do the same, then you will have a very successful business model. You will get checks on a daily basis and you will earn bigger and bigger incentives, which is exactly what you're looking to accomplish!

As a business owner you want to be able to cash out every day and the best way to do that is if you have checks in the mail to take to the bank. Build your business sideways by constantly sampling the water and get as many personal referrals as possible and build your business deep by teaching your distributors to do the same thing.

A Vested Interest In Your Own Success

It is important that you have a vested interest in your own success; otherwise it's never going to happen. What I mean is that you have to invest something of yourself in this business and this project if you expect some kind of return. This is just like anything in life, if you want to be successful; you have to make some sort of investment towards that success.

It's like going to school, if a student does not invest their time, their energy and their effort to doing well, then they often don't. In this business if you don't put in the time, the effort, the energy, and the dedication necessary to succeed, you probably won't. One of the best ways for a person to be successful in this business is for them to create a vested interest for their own success.

They need to do all the things necessary so that they feel there's an investment of themselves in the business so they won't want to quit. If you feel like you have something invested in the business, they are far less likely to give up on it. If they're not invested in their business, they'll feel like they have nothing to lose. If a person has nothing to lose, it makes quitting very easy. I think that a lot of marriages suffer from this these days, which is why so many don't last. The parties have not committed enough of themselves to the relationship to feel there is importance to making it work. I think this is a character flaw that far too many people suffer from these days.

The only way a person can be afraid to lose something is if they feel they have something to lose. When you work at making your business successful, what you would have to lose is all the time, energy, and

NOTES:

dedication invested. While these intangibles don't have a specific price tag associated with them, they definitely have value!! It's important that when you get someone new in the business that you immediately start making them assume an active role in building their business. It's important that they're taking the time to do things in the business, such as going to meetings and delivering the water. Let them invest their time and dedicate part of their life to working this business and they will be investing in their own success and creating value that will make walking away much more difficult!

It's this investment that practically removes quitting as an option. This is why it is so important for you to get your new distributors engaged in creating that vested interest as soon as you can. Each action, each thought, each minute dedicated to the business are the building blocks that create the foundation for a person to continue until they succeed. It's kind of like having a vested interest in your children. I think that the reason most parents love their children isn't so much because they were spawned from their loins, but because the vested interest they have in the success of the child. The time spent teaching them, caring for them, making sure they're safe, helping them learn and all the other things that come with and are important in raising a child.

I think the same aspects are true with the business. The reality is that a parent can have just as much love and care for a step-child as they do for their own child; again it's not because of where they're spawned from, but because of the time put into the betterment and development of the child. There's a very clear correlation between an investment of your time, emotion, and energy and the ultimate success in what you're putting that time towards.

NOTES:

Becoming a Leader

I think that becoming a leader in this project is important for a number of reasons. First and foremost, when you become a leader it will usually lead to greater earning potential for you and for your team members. It stimulates growth and success. People that are serious about the business should do everything in their power to assume a leadership role. Being a leader does not necessarily mean that you are the person that is up on stage at the giant training events. Believe it or not that's not what defines a leader, that simply defines a trainer and they really are not the same thing, although good leaders do get publicly recognized for what they contribute to the program.

Being a leader means that you do what needs to be done to support your prospects, customers and your team. The most effective way to lead is to lead by example. Keep in mind that your people will do what you do; it doesn't matter what you say or what you encourage them to do, they will do what you are doing, it is the example you are providing for them to follow.

If you assume a leadership position and teach leadership by leading, some of your people will follow suit and also start to assume leadership roles. It's not to say that all of your people will, but you will have a much better chance of developing leaders if you are one yourself.

As a leader you should know the fundamentals of this business. The beginning stages of leadership in this project are learning the information and knowing the product. You should know the information and the different things that Enagic® has to offer; the history; the competition; the marketing plan. You should be able

NOTES:

to explain how to sample and effectively utilize the water. You should be able to answer questions and provide guidance. Knowing all of these things is part of becoming a leader; you really need to know the project if you plan on becoming a leader.

The next thing you should do is immerse yourself in the project. To become an effective and successful leader you should surround yourself with the movers and the shakers. Be around the people that are successful, established leaders. Learn from them; study them; be seen with them. It's funny how a person can develop a reputation as a leader simply by being seen with established leaders.

This is part of the way others perceive things. If a leader is hanging out with someone, an outside person will most likely assume that the other person is also a leader. Why else would the known leader be hanging around them? This is not to say that you should become what I refer to as a "leader cling-on". This is a person that will hang out with or befriend a leader, not to improve their own leadership skills, but to enjoy the benefits associating with a leader can bring. Things like free dinners, free drinks, free entertainment, unjustified recognition, unearned influence, undeserved status, etc. Do not become one of these types of people! All it does is label you as is a user, not a leader!

Just remember, if you are an up and coming leader the best way to establish yourself and learn is by being surrounded by people that are already established leaders.

You also need to be there for your team. Sometimes being a leader for your team means working with other teams and opening doors for your people with these other teams, whether or not you get directly compensated for it. Helping distributors from other teams allows you ask for favors when you or your people need them. It creates leverage for you and your team. It also helps to establish a reputation that you are a team player, which often encourages others to want to work with you.

I was asked to help develop a training segment for one of the top Enagic® leaders, Robert Gridelli, for a huge distributor training event. After a bit of discussion we decided that his training topic should be the Fundamentals of Leadership, specifically the qualities that make good leaders. In developing the training I took the word "LEADERS" and assigned a single characteristic for each letter of the word.

L – Loyalty To the project, company, product & your team.
E – Ethical Conduct your business properly & with honor.
A – Attentive Listen to and help with your team's needs.
D – Dependable Be available & follow through.
E – Enthusiasm Be eager to succeed & to help.
R – Respectful To get it, you have to give it.
S – Supportive Assist your team so they can succeed.

If you follow these simply guidelines to being a leader, your results will probably be incredible. Like most things in this project, the principles are simple; the hard part is deciding to do it and then actually doing it!

Remember that in this project the person that helps build the most leaders will ultimately make the most money. Also remember that the best way to do that is to be a leader yourself and to lead by example.

Attending Events: Making the Most of Them

Like everything else in this project, attending events is a process. But before you delve into this, let's define an "event". For the sake of this section of the book, an event is ANY Enagic® or Kangen Water® related gathering. It doesn't matter if it is a small in home presentation, a large weekly meeting, an executive luncheon, a Direct Distributor Training, a Global Online Organization Meeting, a Power Training or some sort of Special Seasonal Event. All of them are important and every person in attendance has a much greater chance for success!

The first thing you will want to do is find out what events are happening each month. There are plenty of different places to find information about events. Talk to your referring distributor and ask them what events are happening and which ones they recommend. If your referring distributor does not know of any, then seek out the information on your own. Remember, you have to become independent as soon as possible, so do not let what someone else doesn't know be your excuse to fail! There are several websites you can visit and a few email lists you can be on that will tell you about meetings in certain areas. Unfortunately, there may not be meetings in all areas, including yours, so you may have to start a meeting yourself, if you want to develop your market.

Once you find your local meetings and trainings, decide which ones you will attend. You should commit yourself to at least one meeting per week and one training per month, and really commit to it! One of the best ways to get the month started is to log in into the Kangen1 Global Online Organization Meeting. This online meeting happens on the first Monday of every month at 7:00 PM PST. Your calendar should have the first

NOTES:

Monday of every month circled and you should be committed to attending all 12 meetings. Then you should circle the rest of the days / dates that you will be attending meetings or trainings. Not only will this serve as a reminder of the meetings you want to attend each month, it will also serve as a guide for when you should be inviting the guests that will attend with you.

While every event is important, we will be mainly covering how to get the most out of attending a live product presentation & product demo, which is the life-blood of the successful distributor. One very important note for this section is regarding attending the presentation. If you invite a guest, attend the presentation with them like you have never seen it before, meaning that you should sit and listen as if you were the new guest. Don't check out your text messages or read your emails on your Blackberry. Don't leave the room and go talk to other distributors. And definitely do not give a presentation from your chair while the speaker is giving their presentation.

I have seen so many distributors that think they are going to impress their guests by saying what the speaker is going to say just a few seconds before he says it. Just to let you know, this does not impress your guest!! All it does is make the presenter less effective and creates a distraction for your guest and those around you. So, for their sake, and yours, please be quite!!

If you invite someone and they don't show, which WILL happen to you, stay and attend the presentation like you have never seen it before. Don't allow a person not showing up to serve as your excuse to not have to attend the presentation. You should want to attend! Make attending another opportunity for you to get

NOTES:
_____

familiar with the project, the presentation and the product. Listen to what the presenter says. Watch how they give the demo and try to pick up their most effective techniques. If you are already at a meeting location, you might as well make the most of it, even when your guest does not show!

The beginnings of the process to make the most out of attending an event is the invitation, but before we get to that, please allow me to discuss one more very important tip for successfully attending events. This is a trade secret that, if you can master, can earn you more money then you ever thought possible! It is a secret that only the best really understand and use effectively, a secret that you should learn!

The secret is to know how to use the monthly events as building blocks to your success. It's to know how to maximize each event and how to build from one to another, with all of your efforts coming together at a main event at the end of the month. Those that understand this strategy and employ it have substantially more success and organizational growth than those that do not. Here is a quick example of what I mean, based on actual meetings.

Every Thursday there is a project presentation and live product demo at the IonFaucet HQ / Orange County National Training Center in Fountain Valley, CA. There is also a big Super Saturday Event the last Saturday of the month at the same location. Here is how I used the meetings to build towards the end of the month event. I invite as many guests as possible to the next Thursday meeting. These might be people I have been sampling that have not seen a presentation; new people I met over the weekend; or even friends or co-workers I have been talking to about the water. I make sure to make my initial invitation a few days before the meeting, Monday or Tuesday is a great day to invite to a Thursday meeting. Inviting them too far in advance of the meeting will allow them the opportunity to forget and make other plans. You want to make sure to follow-up the day of the meeting to make sure they are going to attend. One really great way to ensure they attend is to offer to pick them up.

Okay, back to the meeting. So, I invite a few people and they show up. After the meeting, one of them is expressing real interest, while the other two are just kind of interested. At this point I will turn my focus to the one with the most interest. I will be sure to provide them with fresh samples of water, as well as brochures and other information.

I will also deploy the "anchoring" strategy. This is a simple strategy where I offer to provide extra water for people that they know. When we get to Monday or Tuesday of the next week, I will again have a few direct people that I am inviting, but I will also encourage my person of interest from last week to attend again, but with a few guests of their own. I will then duplicate these efforts for the rest of the month. As the month end draws near, I will make a blanket invitation to ALL of those that have shown interest during the Thursday meetings to attend the Super Saturday event.

This is how I use the weekly meetings to build for the big event at the end of the month. If you do the same, you should see the same type of explosive results that my team has been enjoying for the last several years! When done correctly you should be able to add at least 5 new distributors to your team each month, some directly sponsored by you, some sponsored by your brand new, personally sponsored distributors. All of

NOTES:

them counting for your sales volume, which will move you up the distributor rankings and make you eligible for greater earnings!!

Let's get back to the process that will help you make the most of these live meetings. We will pick back up at the invitation stage of the process. You can invite anyone to a presentation, at any time, but the most effective time is after a person has been sampling the water and seen some kind of result or benefit. The live meeting becomes a way for them to "fill in the blanks" or to take their understanding of the water to the next level.

When extending an invitation you should do it just like you introduce the water, in shot glasses. Just give them as much as they need to say "yes". There are a few things you can do to help improve your chances of a successful invitation. The first is making the right word choice. The word "meeting" can really scare off some folks, so it is a good one to try to avoid. Instead, focus on the aspect of the live product demo. The next thing that can increase your chances is to ask questions that cannot be answered with a "yes" or "no".

The following is a very effective way to invite: "Now that you have been drinking the water for a little while and have had some benefit, you really should experience a live demonstration. There is one this Thursday and I would be glad to pick you up and take you to it. The presenter is awesome and I want to introduce you to him. The presentation starts at 7:30, what time should I pick you up, 6:00 or 6:30?"

Notice that nowhere in the invitation was there a time when a "yes" or "no" question was asked, just a choice of what time to pick them up. I also tossed in a little blurb about the speaker and my desire to introduce

NOTES:

them to this person. Your guest will realize that the speaker is probably a person of some importance and your wanting to introduce them to this person makes your guest feel more important. You should also try to get the person to come to the very next meeting.

There may be a meeting every Thursday, but the meeting THIS Thursday is the one they cannot miss!! Our Thursday meetings are normally conducted by Daniel, who is one of the top producing distributors in the world. So, I tell my guests that the meeting this Thursday is being conducted by one of the top distributors in the world and that they should not miss it. I am making the very next meeting be the one that they should be trying to attend, the only time I am going to tell them that there will be another meeting the following Thursday is if they cannot make this one or at the end of the meeting when I suggest that they think of a few people to invite to the next meeting. If I am going to make the most out of the meetings during the month, I need to have guests at every meeting!

If you notice, my invitation is always based on facts, which is important. If you learn how to "sell" an event, you will have many more attendees. Be honest, just learn how to emphasize the aspects of the meeting that will make it most appealing. As mentioned earlier, make your invitations a few days before the meeting. If you make the invitation too far from the meeting, your guests will most likely forget about it and make other plans. Be sure to follow-up the day before or the day of the meeting. If you are going to pick them up, confirm the time again and DO NOT BE LATE!!!!

If they say they want to meet you for the meeting, it is time for you to employ another trade secret. You will need to know some of the different restaurants around

NOTES:

the area of the meeting in order to effectively use this trade secret. Instead of simply giving them the address to the meeting and telling them to meet you there, ask them to meet you at a nearby restaurant, so you can buy them a cup of coffee or a slice of pie, and so you can tell them a little more before the meeting.

Having them meet you at the restaurant changes the "meeting" into a social gathering. People are far more likely to blow off a meeting than a social invitation. If they don't come to the meeting, they know that there are other people in attendance, so you are not left out in the cold by yourself. Whereas, when they don't show up to a restaurant, they ARE standing YOU up. They ARE leaving YOU out in the cold and alone! This is the reason a person is more likely to show up at the social location before the meeting, they do not want to be rude or socially unacceptable.

If the only way your guest will agree to attend the meeting is for them to meet you at the actual location, then there are a few things you need to do. First, never let your guest arrive at the location before you! If this is a person that likes to be someplace 30 minutes early, then you need to be there 40 minutes early! You NEVER want to allow them to get there first. You want to be able to greet them and show them around. You want their first impression of the meeting to be on YOUR terms, so you have to be there before they arrive.

The next thing is something that you need to NOT do. I call it hovering. Many times when a person is waiting for a guest they will stand out in front of the location, looking down the street or calling their guest to find out where they are. Stop waiting out front!!! Go inside; mingle with the people that are already there; grab a couple of seats at the front of the room. Just don't hover out front.

By standing out front, waiting, you become the unofficial greeter of everyone that shows up before your guest. Unfortunately, when you are waiting for someone, you are the last person that should be greeting other people. You may look upset because they are not there yet. You may be frustrated because they have not picked up their phone. You may look anxious by walking from the front door to the street and looking side-to-side to see if you recognize their car coming down the street. If you look like any of these, you are sending a negative message to the new guests and the other distributors. Go ahead and go inside. If they are going to come, they will call you when they arrive. If they are not going to attend, standing out front is not going to change that fact, so why torment yourself!!

The next step in the process is the "Pre-meeting", which is the time you and your guest are physically together before the meeting starts. While I am referring to this time as the "pre-meeting", a "pre-meeting" is actually the LAST thing you want to be having!! Take the time you have with your guest before the meeting to discuss anything but the water!!! Talk about their life, their kids, wife or husband, plans for the weekend, anything except for Kangen Water®!

You are probably a little confused at this point. Why would I not talk to them about the water at a water meeting? Please allow me to explain. You see, the meetings, at least the Kangen1 meetings, have been put together by very successful people and the entire presentation has been created to provide new guests with the information they need most, in the order that

NOTES:

works the best. You have to understand that every aspect of the meeting has been thought out and that it has a very specific intention. If you ever want to find out specific details of why the presentation is the way it is, you should check out one of the "Training the Trainers Seminars". This is where all the why's to the presentation are explained.

When you start telling your guest about things that will be covered in the presentation you actually weaken the effectiveness of the presentation. It's like having someone tell you all about a movie while you are waiting in line to see it. When you actually get to watching the movie the parts that would have had the most punch are ineffective because you knew they were coming. Giving a pre-meeting has the same effect on your guest. It takes away from the speaker and steals the impact it would have had on your guest. You have to realize that you are not doing yourself or your guest any favors by telling them about what will be covered in the presentation. In fact, you are actually being very counterproductive!

You have no idea how many distributors I hear trying to flex their mental muscles before a presentation. They try to tell their guest everything they can about the water to impress them with their vast aquatic knowledge. In some cases they also give the full preview of the meeting. Not only do they spoil it for their own guest, but for anyone that may be sitting around them. Again, let the presenter do their job by presenting. You do your job by getting your guest to the meeting.

When you and your guest get to the meeting, get yourself good seats. Sit as close to the stage as possible, this helps ensure your guest does not miss any important information. It may also give the speaker

NOTES:

the opportunity to interact directly with your guest, which makes the presentation more memorable for them. Next, get your guest some water! This is a crucial part of the process, especially if they have not been sampling the water. They will need to have as much Kangen Water® in them as possible!! Make sure you tell them where the restrooms are located, as they will need them at some point!

The next thing you want to do is introduce them to some of the other distributors. Make your guest feel at home. If you do not know any of the other distributors, introduce yourself to them, then introduce your guest. Remember, the more comfortable your guest feels, the more receptive they will be to the presentation and information.

The next step in the process is the actual presentation. When the presentation begins, be attentive, to both the presentation and your guest! Pay attention to how much water they have. If they need more, offer to go get it for them. Also pay attention to the presentation. Always watch a presentation like you are seeing it for the first time. Laugh at the jokes, even if you have heard them 100 times before. Raise your hand high if asked to respond to a question.

Be sure that you let the presentation work for you! Don't whisper to your guest during the presentation. Don't check your email messages, text messages or voicemail messages. Don't give the punch line of the jokes that you know are coming before the presenter finishes the joke. Really convince yourself that you are seeing the presentation for the very first time. This will help ensure that you do not do anything to undermine the effectiveness of the presentation!

NOTES:

It is also very important to be respectful to the presenter during a meeting. Don't crack jokes or make comments about the presenter or the presentation. In fact, it is suggested that you "be on your best behavior" during a presentation. It may seem silly for me to put it like this, but you would not believe some of the things I have heard come out of the mouths of distributors during a presentation.

You also want to make sure that your guest is on their "best behavior" as well. Again, it may seem silly for me to have to mention this, but sometimes a guest can really disrupt a presentation. This usually happens when a guest feels compelled to ask a question right in the middle of a presentation. If the presenter is strong and experienced, they can usually handle this type of distraction. However, if the presenter is new to public speaking, having this happen can ruin the presentation. It can quickly become a free-for-all and the presenter can quickly lose control of the room. This is why it is important for YOU to make sure your guest holds any questions or comments until the end of the presentation.

When the presentation has concluded, mingle and talk to a few people with your guest. Let them hear personal stories of the effectiveness of the water or success stories regarding the business. Introduce your guest to the speaker. Answer questions they have or find more experienced distributors to help answer their questions. Stick around for a few minutes after the meeting and make the meeting more meaningful for your guest.

The people that leave immediately following a presentation just don't get it!! They do not understand the potential of the "after-meeting". This is the time that you can assess the interest level of your guest and take

NOTES:

the appropriate action based on the assessment. It is the time you can solidify the interest of your guest by getting 3rd party verification and expert advice. The 10 or 15 minutes immediately following a presentation can actually be the most important part of the entire evening, if you know how to use it!!

The last thing you should do is be prepared for anything at the end of the presentation. Have all the applications you would need for an order, just in case you guest decides they would like to purchase a machine right then and there. Have some brochures or DVD's in case they want to review more information. Have fresh water ready for them to take home. Be ready for anything!

So let's recap the process of making the most out of a meeting:

1. Make your meeting schedule for the month
2. Invite your guests
3. Follow-up
4. Get / meet your guest
5. Pre-meeting
6. Presentation
7. After-meeting
8. Follow-up

These are the simple steps you should follow to make the most of a presentation. Be sure to coordinate with your referring distributor or up-line distributors to maximize the weekly meetings and monthly events. Also watch for special training events! These will help you fine-tune your business and make you a more effective distributor! It is also very important to encourage your own team members to use the weekly meetings, the big monthly events and the training events to build and strengthen their business!

NOTES:

As you move up the ranks in the business you will probably participate in more events. This next section will explain how to set up an event, like an in-home meeting or an Executive Luncheon. As you move up the Enagic distributor ranks, and assume more of a leadership role, it will be important for you to know how to conduct these types of events. Having the ability to host an event allows you to remove restrictions that you may encounter if you have to depend on someone else to make the arrangements.

NOTES:

Conducting Your Own Events

The first thing you need understand is that events are the bread-and-butter of our business. Good events will make you comfortable; bad events will kill your business; and great events will make you a fortune! But before I go much further, let me define an event. An event, in this project, is any gathering of more than three people that will have any aspect of our products or our business discussed. That's it. If you can make this your definition of an event, then you can make every event successful.

An event is a show. It is an orchestrated symphony of intention and presentation that is geared to create a specific response of those that attend. In a great event, nothing happens by accident. Everything is planned. If you intend on creating great events, this is the very first thing that you need to embrace. You've got to take every event seriously and be willing to work hard to make them successful. Your events will be a reflection of your business and your professionalism. Give that the respect it deserves and make every event a show to remember.

NOTES:

Just like a show, a successful event requires a number of different components in order to be successful. You need your stage, your cast of characters, your script, your crew and, of course, you need an audience.

The components just listed are not literal, but they do represent something similar to how they sound. The stage is wherever your presentation is taking place. This could be at someone's home, at an office location, at a restaurant or even at a hotel. Your stage is simply your location.

Your cast of characters are the people that are part of the event: people like the host, the guest presenter, the person that greets the attendees - anyone that will be talking to or dealing directly with the people that make up the audience.

The script is simply what's going to be said. It's the explanation of the company, followed by the live product demonstration and explanation of the machine, followed by the explanation of the business. It is extremely important that the speaker has practiced delivering the information, so it has an effective impact on the audience members.

The people that would represent the crew are any of the people that are there to help make the event run more smoothly. People that are there to help set up the meeting, make sure water is available for the guests, help fill gallons of water for people to take home, help break down and clean up after the meeting. Not to diminish the importance, but basically this is support staff. It's actually the support staff that can be the difference between a bad event, good event and a great one!

NOTES:

The last item that I mentioned, in my list of necessary components for an effective and successful meeting, is the audience. In this list I saved the best for last. I call it the best, because it is the absolute most important item on that list. Without an audience, a show is nothing more than a rehearsal.

In addition to the direct responsibilities of all the people I listed, it is also their responsibility to invite guests and encourage their distributors to attend these meetings so there is an audience. This is part of what they need to do. Everyone involved with organizing any level of event needs to understand that they play a crucial role in the success of that event, not only by making sure that the actual event runs smoothly, but that it is attended by as many people as possible.

The most successful distributors in this project achieved a great deal of their success as a result of the team they were able to assemble. These leaders were able to put together the correct collection of distributors and assigned duties according to the strengths of the individuals. By doing so, they created a group of people that all had their own tasks, but were all focused on the same result. If you expect to get to the point where you can put on your own events, and make them truly successful, that process starts with having the ability to put together a fantastic team.

Now let's look at a few of the specific events that, when put on correctly, can help your business grow tremendously. The first we will look at is the "Press Play Demo".

One of the best ways to get a new distributor going is to encourage them to host a "Press Play Demo". This demonstration approach was actually inspired by top

NOTES:

distributor Robert Gridelli. When he first started in this business, he had no idea how to do a demonstration. But he did know how to load a DVD in and hit play, which is exactly what he did.

Implementing this type of demonstration is extremely easy. The first thing you have the new distributor do is invite some people over to their home. The best people to invite are the new distributor's closest friends and family. The reason for the invitation could be as simple as wanting to share some information and get the opinion.

Then all the new distributor needs is a copy of a demonstration DVD or link to an online version, a DVD player or computer that plays DVD's and a television.

When it's time to start, the new distributor would address the guests and thank them for being there. They would then explain that there is a short video they would like the guests to watch and that afterwards they will be asking for opinions about the information. At that point the new distributor would start the video and head off to the kitchen to start filling gallon bottles for the attendees.

By the time the video is done playing, the bottles should be filled and the new distributor can go back and ask everyone what they thought. Be sure the new distributor knows it is time to listen, not talk. If people have questions, obviously they should be answered, but for this to be truly effective it's best to ask for an opinion and then listen to it. This is an extremely easy approach and an excellent way to get a brand new distributor off and running. The best thing about this approach is that it can be done by anyone at any time. It is not necessary to schedule a full-blown live demonstration with another

NOTES:

distributor, based on their availability. This helps the new distributor immediately gain a sense of independence, which will make them more self-reliant in the future.

As a distributor leader, if you want the press play demo to truly be effective, you need to be willing to provide some of the basic supplies necessary to ensure its success. This includes the demonstration DVD, some basic brochures and gallon bottles for the attendees to take home. It should go without saying, but in order for this to work, the host must be an actual distributor with a machine.

If you decide to recommend the press play demo you should schedule the first one within one week of your new distributor getting their machine. They should plan on conducting a minimum of four press play demos, one each week for four weeks in a row. It should be on the same day each week, so returning guests can already make plans to come back.

Million dollar earnings have been made by distributors that started with this simple, duplicatable approach. Always remember in this business the best way to succeed is by keeping things so simple that anyone can copy them. For whatever reason distributors have the tendency of trying to "improve" things and only end up complicating things. This is exactly the opposite of what you want to do. When it comes to your new distributors, keep it simple, keep it easy and keep it going. These three things will lead to success!

Next we will look at the live home demo. The live home demo is the most effective meeting in this business. There are several reasons that this meeting type is the most effective. First, since the presentation is

NOTES:

happening at someone's home, the attendees are much more comfortable, especially if they've been to the home previously. There's something in this business called a "comfort zone" and most people do not like to be taken out of theirs. If you're looking for initial success, make everything as comfortable as possible for the people attending.

In addition to being more comfortable for the attendees, there is also a major advantage of a home presentation for the host. You see, a meeting in any other location besides your home is one that a person can say they will attend and then never show up. For some reason when a meeting is held at a private residence, it becomes socially unacceptable for a person to agree to attend and then not show up. It is almost like an insult to the host of the presentation. This is one of the reasons that it's highly recommended that one of the first things a new distributor does is organize an in-home meeting.

In addition to the home meeting being the best venue to get people to actually attend, there are a few other reasons to immediately recommend a home meeting to a new distributor. By hosting a home presentation each week for at least a month, the new distributor gets used to conducting live meetings and inviting people to these gatherings. This will help them make the idea of meetings a habit.

The first thing that is vital in a successful event is preparation. You have to be prepared. So when we would do a home presentation, we would start preparing at least an hour and a half beforehand. We would make sure that the equipment was set up and working correctly before the first person ever walked through the door. We would make sure chairs were set up, that all the components of our demonstration were prepared, that there was water made and ready for the people to drink, that there were enough cups, that we had good 11.5 water for the demo, that we had tomatoes, that we had brochures and information for people to take home; we even made sure that the bathroom had toilet paper.

Like I said, you may think some of this seems pretty obvious, but I can tell you, a lot of it gets overlooked. But because we did not overlook these things, our home presentations were extremely effective and created incredible results.

Another reason for the success of our home presentations was the fact that we were working as a team. And as a team we all knew what was expected of us and what our responsibilities were. For example, most of our home presentations were conducted at Daniel's house. I would arrive at Daniel's house about an hour and a half before the presentation was scheduled to start and I would set up the computer, the projector and the screen. All of this would be done and ready to go before the first guest arrived.

I would then stand out front for about 30 to 45 minutes before the presentation would start so that I could greet people. Since a lot of the people that were attending were coming to Daniel's house for the very first time, it made it much easier for them to have someone waiting out front to greet them and let them know they were at the right place. By being out there to greet those people, they were able to start their evening on a very positive note. They felt more at ease knowing they were at the right place and more comfortable by being invited in.

Once people got inside, Daniel and some of the other team members would make them feel at home and get them situated with a glass of water and some casual conversation. Daniel would typically do both the presentation and the demonstration. However, I would be there in a support capacity. When Daniel was in the living room presenting the first part of the presentation, I was in the kitchen setting up the demonstration with all the bottles and the cups. I would arrange all of the components of the demonstration to make getting to them as easy as possible and in the order that they were used during the demonstration.

Once the live demonstration was done and everyone went back into the living room so that Daniel could explain the business aspect of our program, I would break down and put away all of the demonstration components and start filling gallons of water so that when the meeting ended everything was put away, the kitchen was cleaned up and water was ready for people to take home. By making the presentation a team effort we were able to create a very effective use of our time. Remember, your event is put on to create specific results. If you're not creating results, then your events are nothing more than a waste of time.

The next type of event we're going to cover is actually one of my favorites: the Executive Luncheon. An executive luncheon can be an extremely powerful event if coordinated and conducted correctly. I think it is important to mention that the most powerful executive luncheons are closing events, not simply a presentation at a restaurant. A closing event is an event that is orchestrated and scheduled in such a way as to help close new business. I will use our team's monthly executive luncheon as an example for much of the information in this section. Our luncheon was held at the same restaurant and same time each month. Consistency of the location and scheduling is very important if you want people to attend each month.

NOTES:

While the core principles of a live product demonstration and project overview still apply at an executive luncheon, there are some major differences. It is critical to have a team involved with an executive luncheon if you really hope to make it successful.

The first thing you want to do if considering putting on an executive luncheon is finding the correct restaurant. You want to look for a number of different things. The first thing is that the restaurant is nice; if you're going to invite your prospects you want to make sure that venue reflects the professionalism of your business. The next thing you look for is proper size. When you first get started you may only have a dozen or so people attend, which is fine - that's actually how we got started. If possible, you want to find a restaurant that is large enough to accommodate should your executive luncheons start to grow. The last thing you want to do is jump from place to place because you keep outgrowing the restaurants. Once again the aspect of consistency is very important.

Next is when to schedule the executive luncheon. In order to make this a win-win situation for both you and the restaurant owner you should try to schedule your event on their slowest day. By coordinating the event on their slow day for business, you are providing the restaurant with a new source of income on what would normally be a financially slow day. This is obviously a benefit to the restaurant owner. Always be aware of the importance of creating a win-win situation for both the restaurant owner and yourself. If neither party is gaining an advantage, then the effort behind putting this together simply makes no sense.

Now that you have the location and the dates, it is time to organize your team so that you can make the most

NOTES:

out of your executive luncheon. The first detail you want to address is the room configuration or setup. You want the location of where the presenter is set up to be opposite the entrance and, if possible, the restrooms. These two locations will create distractions during the presentation if they are visible to the attendees. You want to eliminate as many distractions as possible so that people will focus on the presentation. The area where the presenter, the screen and the live demo setup are located should also have nothing behind it. Once again, if there is activity in the background, it will become a distraction for the attendees watching the presentation. Also, try your best to position the screen and presenters area so that they can be seen by everyone in attendance.

When we first started our executive luncheons, they were in a smaller section of the restaurant and we did a live demonstration for the attendees. This was easy because the room could only hold about 20 or 30 people, so the regular product demonstration could be conducted and seen by everyone. As our executive luncheon grew, we were forced into a larger section of the restaurant and had to adjust to accommodate for the much larger audience. We accomplished this by using a video camera that was connected directly to the projector. When it was time for the product demo, we simply switched to the video camera and projected close-ups of each part of the demonstration on the screen. This allowed everyone in the room to be able to experience the demo, even when there were 300 people in the room. While you might not need to start doing something like this at the beginning, keep it in mind, so if your executive luncheon grows really big you will have an idea of what to do to keep the demo effective.

NOTES:

One thing I should mention is that if you decide you're going to pursue larger events like executive luncheons, you need to be prepared to invest resources into the proper type of equipment. This could include laptop computers, projectors, video cameras, a speaker system and maybe a microphone system. Also keep in mind that if you get this equipment, you will need someone who knows how to use it. So keep an eye out for members of your team that are more technologically savvy.

For a really effective executive luncheon, you will need a team to help. There should be at least two people that are taking care of the front door. One should be handling the ticket sales and collection of money, and the other should be acting like a doorman, keeping people out until it's time for them to be seated. This actually leads us to another insider tip that will help your event be more effective. It is extremely important that no one attending the executive luncheon be allowed into the restaurant until everything is set up and no earlier than 30 minutes before the start of the event. Let your attendees gather outside and create a crowd of people. As people start to talk, a buzz of energy will start to surge through the crowd, which will increase the level of excitement outside and will then transfer once the people come inside.

A lot of people ask if they should keep their executive luncheons private or if they should allow outside teams to also attend. Pay very close attention to the next few sentences! You absolutely, positively want to allow other teams to attend your executive luncheons. The tickets they buy help your team members attend for free.

When you initially set up your executive luncheon, you'll be negotiating with the owner of the restaurant to get a

NOTES:

price that is fair to him or her and to the attendees. Just so you know, any sort of buffet is usually best. It offers the widest variety, the easiest access and usually the lowest price of any restaurant option. If the restaurant does not offer a buffet, then it is best to offer a single-item menu with something like chicken. If you do this, also be sure to offer some sort of vegetarian alternative.

Since you are helping the restaurant gain more business, you do have the right to negotiate the price. Ultimately, what you are trying to achieve is the ability to have all of your own team members attend this event absolutely free. The only way you can do this is by having the costs associated with your team members being at the luncheon offset by an overage that is created by the paid tickets purchased by outside team members.

It is important to keep the cost reasonable. We found that a $15-$20 per ticket price point is usually best. You want the ticket price to be approximately $5 more than the actual cost being paid to the restaurant per person. This is what will allow you to build the extra money needed to cover your people. Let's say that you've worked out with the restaurant that each person will cost a total of $10 for their lunch. Based on this price, you charge $15 per ticket. This means for every two outside team members that attend your executive luncheon, one of your team members attends for free.

When it comes to free access to your team, the best rule of thumb is to allow access based on distributor ranking. Start by letting the newest distributors in first, for free. If you are able to allow higher ranking distributors in for free also, that is great! But understand that your higher ranking distributors earn more money for doing the same work, so they should have more available resources for things like attending an executive luncheon; they will need to step up eventually.

By following this model, if you hosted an executive luncheon that had a total of 50 people attend, 30 people from outside groups and 20 of your distributors and their guests, 15 of the 20 would be able to have lunch and be part of the event at no cost to you or to them. This is why it is so important to make an event like an executive luncheon open to outside groups. In fact, you want your executive luncheon to be so beneficial that everybody wants to attend! Because the more people that attend from outside groups, the more of your people that can attend for free. Just be sure the ratio of outside distributors to your team stays about even!

When it comes time to start seating people, you want to have someone designated to do this job: the "greeter and seater". This person is the first official contact that every attendee will have at the executive luncheon. So this person should be cheery and welcoming. They need to know who is who and where each group is sitting. The most successful executive luncheons are not a "free-for-all". It is not open seating. It is not first-come, first-served. If you are organizing the event, then your distributors come first; they get the best seats and yes, they do receive preferential treatment.

At our events we sometimes get people from outside of our group that end up having a problem with the fact that this is the way we conduct things. Our response is simple and straightforward, but respectful. We tell them that this is not a company-sponsored event, so our direct team members are seated first and if they're not happy with it, they are more than welcome to go out and coordinate their own event. And if anyone still has a problem with it, we are more than happy to give them

NOTES:

their money back and send them on their way. Just for your information, no one ever ends up leaving!

To help make things move more smoothly, you'll want to have your distributor leaders gather their groups together and have them ready to enter. When it is their turn to enter, the group leader needs to lead the group. This person will help make sure everyone gets in, gets their ticket to the appropriate person, makes their way to their seats and gets everybody situated.

Another important part of the seating process is music. You have to have music playing before people walk through the door. The music literally sets the tone. It creates a vibe, it sets the pace and it forces the energy in the room to increase. The music should be playing just louder than a normal conversation, which will force people to speak louder. This increase in the volume of everyone's voices creates energy in the room. If someone asks you if you can turn down the music, you politely say no. If they respond saying they can't hear each other when they're talking, you tell them that is great, the volume of music is perfect and doing exactly what it is supposed to.

If the restaurant has a house audio system, use it to play your music. But if the restaurant does not have an audio system, you need to have your own. There have been times where we've used our own audio system for our music. The only downfall this creates is that the volume of the music is not consistent throughout the restaurant. People closest to the speakers hear them the loudest and for those at the back of the room, it is much less. When using our speaker system I have had people that were sitting in the very front come up to me and complain that the music was too loud.

NOTES:

Let's put this in perspective; that would be like going to a live musical, sitting in the front row and then complaining that the orchestra was too loud. It's part of the show. My response was simple. I told him I was sorry if the music was too loud for him, and that I would gladly get him a seat in the back of the room where the volume of the music would not be so high. He went back to his front row seat, and the volume of the music stayed right where it was.

One more thing that can really add some life to an executive luncheon is having someone taking pictures. Most people love to have their picture taken. They like to laugh, smile and be made the center of attention, if even for just a few seconds. Start by going around the inside and outside of the restaurant taking "action" shots of people arriving and being seated. Then take a few pictures during the actual presentation and demonstration. But it is extremely important that they not create a distraction for the audience. The best thing to do is take pictures from the back of the room of the entire group. If they want to take pictures of just the presenter, do so using the zoom, again, from the back of the room.

The best pictures are going to come after the presentation and while people are eating. This is when the person taking the pictures should "float" around the room. They should go from table to table taking pictures of groups, parties of two, three and four, and individual pictures of some of the group leaders. The person taking pictures needs to have an extremely outgoing personality. They should encourage people to be energetic; do things like lift their water glasses as if to propose a toast. Remember, these pictures may end up at some big event someday. So make sure that the

NOTES:

pictures being taken are worthy of ending up in an event!

These are the main points of an executive luncheon. You have to remember that the real power of the executive luncheon is doing it correctly and then having the time for people to talk, ask questions and listen to other people after the presentation. An executive luncheon creates the opportunity for new prospects to stick around for a little while. This allows them to get the type of information they will need to make a buying decision. This is the true power of an executive luncheon and is the reason you should want to host your own.

The Payment Process – Take It Step-By-Step

This next section contains some of the most important information in this entire book, so I am going to ask you to pay close attention, use the notes area at the bottom and really absorb the information.

The "payment process" does not refer to the way that the customer is going to pay for their purchase, at least not directly. It refers to the process that you should use with every single person that says the words "I'd like to buy one of these machines". Each step in the process is actually a different payment option for the prospect and it is important to present them in a specific order and manner.

As soon as you hear a prospect say this, it is immediately time for you to start the process. As with every other process we have discussed, there are several steps and you do not go to step 3 until steps 1 and 2 are completed. So, always start with step 1 and, if necessary, move on to the next step.

This process will determine which payment option will be right for your prospect and this decision will have an effect on you, so learn to take them through the process and when they have arrived at the option that is right for them, you are done! Shut up!! Don't give them any more options!!!

The first option is for them to pay cash, and I mean cash, like actual dollar bills. There are some people that prefer to pay with cash, so this is where we start. The way that I approach the first step in the process is with humor. As soon as a prospect tells me that they are ready to purchase a machine I will immediately reply with, "That's great! Will that be $100's or $50's?" Most

NOTES:

of the time, like 99 times out of 100, the response I get is the prospect saying, "yeah, right!" However, there is that 1 in 100 that will tell you that it will be $100's or it will be $50's, indicating that they intend on paying for the machine with cash. As soon as I hear that they want to pay cash, the purchase options are DONE! The payment process for this customer is completed! There is no reason for me to give any other options; they have told me which one they want!

Most of the time this first step is immediately followed by step 2, but it is important that you go through every step with every prospect and that you start with step 1. DO NOT pre-judge someone thinking that they cannot afford to pay cash. Let them tell you! You may actually be surprised by those that will pay cash and those that won't!!

On to step 2. So now the prospect has said, "yeah, right!" and I immediately counter with a small chuckle and say, "I'm only kidding, here is what most people are doing..." I then go into the option of using a credit card or multiple credit cards to make the purchase. At this point I want to be sure to tell the prospect some of the benefits of using a credit card, like having the flexibility of paying a minimum payment if necessary or earning points or miles by using a credit card with a reward program.

This is the option that many prospects choose, so, if they say that they want to use their credit card, the purchase options are DONE! The payment process for this customer is completed! There is no reason for me to give any other options; they have told me which one they want!

NOTES:

If they tell me that they do not have a credit card or one or more with a high enough available balance, then it is on to Step 3.

This next step is presenting the idea of using their current financial institution or an outside financing company to fund the purchase, basically them applying for a personal loan to purchase the machine. This step can be a little tricky, as you are going to have to ask about the prospects personal credit worthiness. Those that think this may be an option will usually have no problem entertaining the idea, but if you run across someone that immediately responds with "I don't think that will work" or any variation of that, they probably have some credit issues and are trying to save embarrassment by not going there. RESPECT this and move on! The last thing you want to do is to make your prospect feel uncomfortable!

If the Step 3 option seems like it might work, then point them in the right direction to review some of the different plans we have found or encourage them to contact their own financial institution to see about a personal line of credit. What you MUST NOT DO is collect their information and then apply for credit somewhere for them. Doing this is a form of fraud and it can have very serious consequences, including having your distributorship revoked! Play it straight and allow your prospect to apply for themselves. You just point them in the right direction if they need an option other than their own bank or financial institution.

If the outside financing option will not work, then it is on to Step 4, the Enagic® in house financing program, Enagic® Credit System (ECS). For those not able to utilize one of the first 3 options this is usually the one they choose, but be sure to explain the way it works in

NOTES:

complete detail. In case you don't know, here is how the ECS program works.

The customer has 4 different options for the duration of their payments; 3 payment option, 6 payment option, 10 payment option and 16 payment option. Note: some of the lower priced machines do not offer the 16 month option. There is an installment charge of $10 for every month, so choosing the 16 month option will add an extra $160 to the purchase price. If you are in an area that charges sales tax, then the sales tax will be calculated and added to the total amount of the down payment. If the machine is going to be shipped, then a $23 shipping fee will be added to the total down payment. Then there is a deposit on the actual machine. The deposit for an SD501 is $380.00. The deposit is also added to the total down payment. These four things add up to make the total down payment that must be made. For example, an SD501 using the 16 month option purchased in Torrance, CA will require a total down payment of $921.20. This is $160 installment charge, $358.20 sales tax, $23 shipping fee and the $380 deposit, some of these figures are subject to change.

The monthly payments for the machine must come from an automatically deducted source, either a credit card or a checking account. The monthly payment for the SD501 using the 16 month payment option is $225.00 per month. Just recently Enagic® added additional payment options which will allow a buyer to extend payments for as long as 24 months. While the in house option is good to have for those who need it, it does have some draw backs, both for you and the customer.

The drawback for you is that if the prospect uses the ECS, you will only be paid the Special Bonus points upfront. The balance of the commission will be paid

NOTES:

after the machine has been paid off. Here is an example of what I mean
.

Let's say that your prospect Sally decides she want to purchase an SD501 and that she is going to make 16 payments using the ECS. Sally will be a 3A sale for you. When she makes her purchase, you will receive a commission for $150, which is 3 special bonus points of $50 each. The remainder of the commission, $705.00, will be paid to you when she is done paying off her machine in 16 months.

Having a small percentage of ECS purchases in your group can actually be beneficial, as it creates a stream of income down the road. Unfortunately, having too many ECS deals in your group can make things difficult, especially as you are just getting started. This is one of the main reasons you should learn the payment process and use it the same way every time. I will share a story with you about this, but before I do, let me finish with the drawbacks of the ECS program.

The drawback for the distributor is pretty obvious, but there are also drawbacks for the prospect. The first, and usually the biggest, is the down payment. An ECS purchase requires the down payment which, depending on the state of purchase, can be over $900.00. This up-front payment can be an obstacle for some people. Then there is the monthly payment. It is an automatic withdraw every month; same date, same amount. There is no flexibility and no control for the buyer. Let's be real, sometimes things happen and we need a few extra days to be able to send off that payment for a bill. Using the ECS you do not have that flexibility and when the time comes the money goes!

NOTES:

Let me get back to the story I mentioned about the ECS program. I know a distributor that was doing pretty well with making sales, however when his prospects said they were ready to buy, the first thing he asked was if they wanted to use the Enagic® payment program. Part of this was because he did not take himself out of the purchase equation, which I will explain shortly. What ended up happening is the majority of his sales ended up being ECS deals, which would not be so bad, except that in not following the payment process he ended up teaching his prospects to do the same thing as him. So when he had buyers that decided to be distributors, they, too, brought up the ECS program as soon as someone indicated they were ready to buy.

What he ended up with was a group full of sales that paid him VERY LITTLE upfront. Now 16 months into being a distributor some of the pay offs started to hit and the larger balanced of commissions started to come in, but it was pretty rough for this individual for the first year and a half. If you can keep your ECS deals down to about 20% - 25% of your total sales, you should be pretty good. The other distributor had over 70% of his sales with the ECS program and it made his early days as a distributor very difficult, even though he and his team were making a good amount of sales.

There is one more option available, but I am going to ask you to discuss this option with your sponsor or the leader you are working with. It is an option that looks good on paper, but that is very difficult to make work, so I will not go into too much detail about it. It is a program called the Tokurei, just so you know the name so you can ask your sponsor. In very rare cases this is a great program for someone, but 999 times out of 1000 it does not work out and it ends up being a waste of time and

NOTES:

effort. While you should know about it, I personally do not promote it much!

Taking Yourself Out of the Purchase Equation

In the previous section I shared the story of an Enagic® distributor and I mentioned that he did not take himself out of the purchase equation. Please allow me to explain what I mean and why this is very important.

When the distributor in the previous section made his sales he assumed that every person he spoke to would be in the same financial situation as him. He figured that since he had to use the ECS program to buy his machine that they would need to use it to buy theirs.

In some cases I am sure he was correct, but this couldn't be true for all the people that eventually bought from him. He failed to take himself out of the purchase equation of someone else. Making the assumption that they would need to use the ECS program had him going straight to it as the first option. By doing this he created a habit for himself and for his future distributors, a habit that ended up making life as an Enagic® distributor very difficult for him.

No matter what your personal situation might be, you must take yourself out of the purchase equation of another person! An easy way to do this is to learn the steps of the Payment Process and to always go through them exactly the same way, every time. Having a process created by someone else helps protect you against making your own process based on you and your circumstances.

Remember, simple steps and processes are what make success here. Learn them, follow them and teach them. This is the best way to ensure that your experience as an Enagic® distributor is enjoyable and rewarding!

NOTES:

Distributor Essentials

I guess the easiest way to explain distributor essentials is to say that they are the topics that don't really fit into a main category, however, they are very important and distributors really need to understand them. In this section we will cover a few different distributor essential topics.

UNDERSTANDING THIS INDUSTRY

The first topic we will cover is this industry. While most people think they have an understanding of the industry we are in, the same people really don't understand the complexity that this industry can present. Let's start by taking a look at what we are, and what we are not.

This is a direct sales program, meaning that we, as distributors, market and sell products directly to the end-user. That's what direct sales actually means. Now, because the unique Enagic® distributor compensation plan includes an override structure, certain people have pulled the project out of the area of direct sales and lumped it into the network marketing and multilevel marketing industry. I am not saying there is anything wrong with network marketing or multilevel marketing, although both have had companies with questionable reputations, but our project really is not either of those. It is direct sales.

Because this project has been lumped in with network marketing and multilevel marketing programs, sometimes people prejudge what we actually do. They go off of rumors, misconceptions and mudslinging campaigns created to discredit and undermine our project.

NOTES:

Unfortunately, many of the people associated with this business, perpetuate this misunderstanding by using terminology normally associated with the network marketing and multilevel marketing industries. One of the best ways for distributors to help stop these misunderstandings is to stop using this type of terminology when explaining our business.

Terms like sponsor, down-line and even meeting, are all terms widely used in network marketing and multilevel marketing. They are also used in our project. By simply using some other words to explain our business we can separate ourselves from the negative connotation and stereotypes connected to the network and multilevel marketing industry.

Instead of using the word sponsor, you could use the word referrer, since you are describing the person that referred you to this business. Instead of using the word down-line, you could call it your sales group, since you are describing the group of distributors that are making sales on their own behalf as well as on your behalf. Instead of using the word meeting, you could call it a live product demonstration or a project overview. By simply changing the way we explain this business, we can help keep this project from being lumped into the network marketing or multilevel marketing industry.

The reason this becomes important is because one of the things that the competition does is attacks our marketing method, saying that we are a network marketing company, which is the reason our products are more expensive. An uninformed consumer may believe this to be true. We all know that this is not true, that our products are more expensive because they are the best in the industry. A premium product comes with a premium price, which is a basic consumer fact. But to

NOTES: _____

an unknowing consumer that is easily influenced, the argument that our products are overpriced because we are a network marketing company has convinced some people to purchase other ionizer brands.

This is why distributors need to assume some responsibility in reducing the perception that our project is a network marketing company or a multilevel marketing company. We need to educate consumers to the fact that we are a direct sales company and we need to make sure they truly understand what that means.

There something else that is important for distributors to understand. Since our project is often mistaken for a network marketing or multilevel marketing program, sometimes it attracts people with what I refer to as a "Network Marketing" mentality. These are people that try to turn this opportunity into a way to make some fast money. They typically are not in it for the long haul and they're ready to jump to another program should it seem that it has more to offer. They are really not interested in building a business with this project; they just look for a quick buck.

The problem with people with this type of mentality is that they do not care if they have a negative impact or even destroy the businesses that other people have created. It is very important that you warn your distributors to watch out for people like this. These people prey on new, inexperienced distributors and distributors that are still trying to establish themselves in this project. These are the people that are the most susceptible to the network marketing minded person.

Distributors need to use caution if they are ever approached with some other type of business opportunity or moneymaking deal. This is not to say that

NOTES:

a person cannot be diversified in their business dealings. It is more to say that if you decide to commit to this project, you should truly commit to it and give it the chance to become the thriving business it has the potential to be. Unfortunately, some of the network minded individuals convince both newer and establish distributors that the grass is greener somewhere else.

Just remember that the Enagic® business is a real business opportunity, where some of these other programs are nothing more than get rich schemes. One of the easiest ways to tell the difference is the way the project is promoted. In most cases a real business will lead with what they have to offer, which, in our case, are the best water ionizers in the industry. Many times these other projects will lead with the promise of money, the allure of flashy cars and the idea of a carefree, extravagant lifestyle. There is one rule in business that people should keep in mind if approached by someone offering easy money and the opportunity of a lifetime. Easy money normally comes at a very hard price!

If you can remember this and teach your distributors to also remember this, both you and they will be much better off in the long run. If you are able to understand this industry, you'll be able to make the most of it and not be taken advantage of by those who would abuse it.

KNOWING YOUR MACHINE

Our next topic in the distributor essentials section is knowing your machine. It is important that a distributor not only be comfortable with their machine but also be proficient in using it. The more you use your machine, the more you use a different grades of waters, the more you learn how these waters work and the more you make the machine part of your daily life the more you

NOTES:
_____

will ultimately get out of your investment in a water ionizer.

In this section we will cover a few tips and hints on how to get the most out of your machine.

First, let's talk about pre-filters. This is something that many distributors ask about. Using a pre-filter is completely up to the end user. Personally, I recommend that distributors at least consider a pre-filter, as it will increase the quality of the water, will extend the life of the internal filter and will generally help your machine last longer.

There are a number of different pre-filters available, for all types of source water. Each of these can be very different, so is important to do some research to find out which one will work best. For just a general pre-filter I recommend a two-stage filter, with the sediment filter and a KDF filter. KDF is a material used to filter many things out of tap water. If you're going to use a KDF filter, I recommend using one with at least 1 pound of KDF material.

Next, let's talk about some machine basics. One of the things that seems to get new distributors and users confused at the beginning of using a machine is the automatic cleaning feature. When the machine has been run for a total of 15 minutes or more, either continuous or accumulated, and then is stopped, the machine will go into an automatic cleaning cycle. This cycle lasts for 30 seconds. During this time the machine's power must be on and water must be flowing to the machine. If water is not flowing through the machine, then the cleaning cycle is not happening.

NOTES:

It should also be noted that if water is not run through a machine for longer than 24 hours, as soon as you turn the machine on it will go into a cleaning cycle. This is a precautionary feature to ensure that any trace water that may have remained in the machine is flushed out prior to making new drinking water. While the machine is in the automatic cleaning mode it will beep, a red light will flash on the front of the machine and it will say "CLEANS" on the display screen.

This brings us to the next point which is water flow. You will quickly learn that one of the ways to increase the alkalinity of the water produced by the machine is to reduce the water flow. While this might seem like a good idea, it is not! Running the water slowly can make the water too alkaline, which can make it taste fishy and very unpleasant. Running the water slowly also hinders the internal filter from working the way it was designed to work. You need to run the water at a full flow. You can test your pH levels using drops and adjust the flow slightly to ensure you are getting strong and effective alkaline water. But just make sure you're not running the water too slowly. I may have actually mentioned water flow previously in another section, but I thought it was important enough to mention it one more time.

The next tip is about the volume of the voice prompts. Many people do not know they can adjust the volume level of the voice prompt of their SD501, or turn it off entirely. All you have to do is turn the power off on your machine, then, while it is still plugged in, press and hold the alkaline water button, which says "Kangen". After a few seconds the machine will power up and the display screen will reflect the current volume setting, which is either Off, Low or High.

NOTES:

To change to a different setting, simply press the "Kangen" button. It will toggle through the different choices. Once you have it set to the desired volume level, all you have to do is hit the power button, which will turn the machine off. When you hit the power button once more, the machine will turn back on and the volume will be at the level you set it.

Our next machine tip is about making the 11.5 pH Strong Kangen Water. Some people have a hard time making 11.5 pH water, which is the water that is able to emulsify cooking oil, as is sometimes demonstrated in live product demos. First off, everyone that uses a water ionizer has to understand that the machine is programmed based on certain parameters. The first, and probably the most important, is that the machine works under the assumption that the source water entering the machine has a pH level of around 7, which is considered neutral.

If the source water entering the machine has a pH level that is lower than 7, it will probably not be able to make 11.5 pH water. And the opposite is also true, if the source water has a pH level that is higher than 7, the machine will probably not be able to make the 2.5 pH Strong Acidic Water. Well water is typically the most common water with a different pH level, which is why Enagic® offers to calibrate machines that are being used with well water.

Doing a quick test of a new client's water before they purchase their machine is always a good idea. Just get some of their normal tap water in a cup and use the pH drops. If everything is correct, the drops should turn the water an aquamarine color. However, if the water turns a very light green or yellowish, it may be too acidic, and if it turns dark blue or light purple, it may be

NOTES:

too alkaline. If either of these happens, it is advised that you consult with Enagic® when processing the machine order to see if special calibration is necessary. As long as the source water is neutral, you should be able to make both the 11.5 pH and 2.5 pH waters.

Here are a few helpful hints that will help ensure that when you make these grades of water, they are as good as they can get. Start by making sure that the enhancer fluid tank is filled and securely in place. Sometimes salt deposits can build up around the intake port, which can clog the injection of the saline solution. Just make sure that the enhancer fluid tank is clean and that where it connects to the machine is clear of any salt residue.

Next, turn the machine on to one of the alkaline water settings and start running the water. You'll want to make sure that the water is flowing very fast. With the machine set to the alkaline water setting and with the water running press the "Strong Acid" button on the machine, this is the orange colored bottom button on the control panel. Keep the water flowing fast until the machine indicates the water needs to be turned down. It will do this by saying "decrease flow" and the display panel will say "OVER FLOW". At this point go ahead and turn the water flow down until the stream from the white hose starts to braid, which means it is not a steady stream anymore. If your water pressure is not high enough to set off the Over Flow alarm, then go ahead and just follow the instructions as if it did.

When making these grades of water, the top white hose is where the 11.5 pH water exits. The gray hose or pipe coming from the bottom of the machine is where the 2.5 pH water exits. You want to be sure to capture both of these waters in different containers. There are two simple ways to test to see if the water being produced is

NOTES: _____
_____

strong. Number one is to test the 11.5 pH water. Take your thumb and index finger and rub them together under the water coming out of the top white hose. For most people their fingers will start to feel slick as they are rubbed together. This is caused from the oils on the fingertips being emulsified by the 11.5 pH water. Some people with extremely dry skin will not be able to do this as they simply do not have enough oil on their fingertips for it to be emulsified.

The other way you can check to make sure the waters being produced are strong is to capture some of the 2.5 pH water in a glass and smell it. If it has a very strong odor, like that of chlorine, then you are making some very good quality 2.5 pH water. It is important to note that when making the 11.5 pH and 2.5 pH waters that the container capturing the 2.5 pH water be lower than the bottom of the machine. If the container capturing this water is elevated the water can remix in electrolysis chamber with the 11.5 pH water which will make it so neither grade works the way it was intended.

One more important thing to remember about 11.5 pH water is that it needs to sit for a few days before it is at full strength. So be sure to give it a few days before trying to emulsify oil. It will be strong enough to remove the oil-based pesticides on most fruits and vegetables, but it does need to sit for a few days to gain strength if you're going to use it for demonstration purposes. Also with the 2.5 pH water, be sure that the lid of the container that it is in is fastened tightly.

TOOLS AND RESOURCES

The next section of the distributor essentials will concentrate on distributor tools and resources. There are numerous different tools and resources available,

NOTES:

and you will find that different distributors have different preferences. We will cover some of the specific tools that we recommend, but we do suggest that each distributor checks into the different tools that are available in order to find what will work best for them. One excellent way to start is to ask successful, established distributors what tools they prefer.

The first resource we recommend becoming very familiar with is the Enagic® company website, www.enagic.com. This website is filled with all sorts of information and should be a location visited by distributors at least a few times a week. Remember that as an independent distributor the company website is also, in a way, your website, so use it!

If you decide that you would actually like to have your own website then we recommend that EWS, Enagic® Web Systems, replicated websites. There is also an excellent blog service provided by Enagic®. Each of these allows a distributor to have their own personal web presence and gives them the ability to promote their business using the Internet. There is a cost to subscribe to both of these services. If this is something you are interested in you should talk to your Referrer to find out more.

When I first started with Enagic® I identified the need for a distributor resource website. I recognized that there was information spread all over the Internet about our products, but there was no single location that brought it all together. In order to fill this void I introduced a free distributor resource website, which received over a million hits in just the first few years it was available. The old website was recently replaced with a new free resource website, www.going6a.com, which offers even more, including a library of professionally produced

NOTES:

- 233 -

videos. There are also numerous tools available, including the Visual Impact (VI) Bottles. These 32 oz bottles have been designed to create instant interest. The flagship bottle has been designed to resemble a standard AA battery. Since most people are only familiar with the term "alkaline" in regards to a battery, I figured why not go with what people are familiar with? The two unique designs are professional and eye catching and will get the conversation started for you, which is something most distributors look for in a marketing tool.

Another useful resource is the Water Is Life reusable water bag. These bags are by far the best option for providing water samples. They are easy to store, are designed to promote the properties of the water and they hold the properties better than just about any other option.

I highly recommend that any distributor who is serious about success in this business visits these sites and utilize the information they provides.

The next website that we recommend is the www.ionfaucet.com website. This site offers some of the best brochures, DVDs and project tools and resources available in this business. In addition to marketing materials and other tools, this website also offers a variety of aftermarket accessories that will enhance the look and function of the machine. Some of these accessories eliminate the need for the hoses that are normally connected to the faucet, while others create a custom housing for the machine. It is important that you become familiar with the different types of options that are available; as your prospects may be interested in a more sleek and streamlined look when their machine is installed.

NOTES:

MOVING UP THE ENAGIC® DISTRIBUTOR RANKS

The next distributor essential that we will cover deals with the ranking system in the Enagic® business. There seems to be quite a bit of confusion when it comes to this topic, which is why we've included it.

Most of the confusion about this topic comes from people trying to make it more complicated than it has to be. The distributor ranking in this program is very easy to understand if you do not try to complicate things.

First we'll start with the point system. The Enagic® distributor compensation plan is built on a system of points, not levels. Each sale has a total of eight points that are paid out. The point payout starts at the point-of-sale, meaning with the person that actually made the sale. Points then work their way up to the distributors connected with the seller, until all the points are used up.

This is where it can get complicated if you let it. But you don't have to let it! It is simple subtraction, starting with eight points and then subtracting the amount of points each person is entitled to, until the points are all gone. How many points a person is entitled to will depend on their distributor ranking, and the lane in which the sale was made.

Let's back up for a moment. Let's first identify the different ranks and then I can give an example of the way the points are paid out. The ranks go 1A to 6A, with the number indicating the maximum amount of points that that person is eligible for in that lane and the "A" stands for agent. So a 5A, would be defined as a five point agent, eligible for a maximum of five points in their five-point lane.

NOTES:

Each distributor must complete two personal 1A sales, this establishes the foundation of their sales group and they are now allowed to start moving up the distributor ranks. If any distributors are developed from those first two sales, the maximum override for the original distributor would be one point. We will provide some examples using a distributor named Bob.

Once Bob makes his first two 1A sales, his advancement is based on either personal sales or group sales or a combination of both. In either event, advancement to the next higher ranking only comes with a personal sale, meaning that even if Bob has enough sales volume within his group to be eligible for advancement, he must make a personal sale in order for it to activate. If Bob were to make a third personal sale, that sale could be registered as a 2A lane, meaning that Bob would receive two points on the personal sale and a maximum of two points on overrides from that sales lane.

The next advancement comes at 10 sales. These can either be personal sales or sales made within his sales group or a combination of both. Once Bob has at least 10 sales his next sale activates his status as a 3A distributor, meaning that Bob would receive three points on his own personal sale and a maximum of three points on overrides from that sales lane.

The next advancement comes at 20 sales. Again these can either be personal sales or sales made within his sales group or a combination of both. Once Bob has accumulated at least 20 sales, his next sale activates his status as a 4A distributor, meaning that Bob would receive four points on his personal sale and a maximum of four points on overrides from that sales lane.

NOTES:

The next advancement comes at 50 sales. Once again, these can either be personal sales or sales made within his sales group or a combination of both. Once Bob has accumulated at least 50 sales, his next personal sale activates his status as a 5A distributor, meaning that Bob would receive five points from his personal sale and a maximum of five points on overrides from that sales lane.

The last advancement of the distributor ranking comes at 100 sales. As before, these can either be personal sales or sales made within his sales group or a combination of both. Once Bob has accumulated at least 100 sales, his next personal sale activates his 6A distributor ranking, meaning that Bob would receive six points from that personal sale and a maximum of six points on overrides from that sales lane.

It is important to note that each sales lane acts and works independently of each other; meaning that Bob's 3A sales lane and a 5A sales lane have nothing to do with each other.

Here is an example of the way the point system pays out.

Let's say that Bob is currently a 5A and he has a distributor in his 5A lane that has a total of 10 sales in his own developing sales group. We will call him Jim. Jim has a brand-new sale, which will activate his 3A distributor status. As such Jim receives three points from the sale. The next person in line would be Bob. Because Jim was in Bob's 5A lane, Bob is eligible for a maximum of five points on the override from Jim's sale. We started with eight points; Jim was eligible for three of those points, which leaves the remaining five points being paid to Bob. That is the way the payout happens.

NOTES:

Obviously there are numerous variations of to whom and how much is paid, but it all depends on their distributor ranking and the ranking of the sales lane.

The easiest way to not get confused by the ranking system is to simply make personal sales and help your developing distributors to also make personal sales. Enagic® will guide a distributor through the ranking system and will let them know when they have achieved a higher ranking.

UNDERSTANDING COMMISSION REPORTS

The next subject we will address in the distributor essentials section is, understanding the commission reports. As you start moving up the distributor ranks you will probably want to see sales reports so you can track your progress and monitor your group.

You do this by making a genealogy request on the distributor section of the Enagic® website. Once a request is made, your genealogy report will be e-mailed to you. The report contains detailed information on sales within your personal sales group. This report includes any sales within the eight point structure of your sales group. Sales made outside of your eight point structure can be reviewed by requesting a 6A Education Allowance report. Please note that you must be at least a 6A in order to request this report.

Once you receive your report you want to know how to read it, that is what will be covering in this final section of the distributor essentials. The report reads from left to right and each line represents an individual sale. You may find that two lines seem to have almost identical information. That is an indication that that particular

NOTES:
_____

sale was made using Enagic's® in-house financing plan. But before we get to that, let's start at the beginning.

The first thing you'll come to on the first line of your report is the number of the sale. Your first sale will start with the number one. Next in line is the date the machine was sold. The date code starts with the year, followed by the month, followed by the day the machine was purchased. Immediately following the date is the customer or distributor ID along with part of the purchaser's name. Immediately following their name is the current distributor ranking of that buyer.

The next box and the line indicate which product was purchased. Immediately following that is a number. That number indicates the number of points that that buyer represents for you. Meaning that if a one is in the box following the product; it means that you received one point from that product sale.

The next eight sections contain the top eight distributors within your group that you personally sold and their subsequent sales. The sales will be listed with monetary values based on how much you either received or will receive from each sale. The ninth section includes all the others within your personal sales group.

As mentioned before, if the name appears on two separate lines it means that that buyer used the Enagic® in-house financing plan. If this is the case there will be two dollar figures listed, the first will be the special bonus points you received immediately following the sale. The amount listed on the second line will be the balance that you will receive once the machine has been paid off.

NOTES:

Immediately following this information is the accumulated amount you have earned through your personal sales and your group sales overrides. These are listed with all monies earned, whether they have been received or not. Next to the accumulated amounts is the "Paid" section. This section contains dates. The date indicates when the commission check was paid for that particular sale.

In some cases, there will be a blank space for the date a commission was paid on the balance of an Enagic® in-house finance purchase. This means one of two things, either the machine is still being paid off or the machine payoff is past due and there is a remaining balance. When this happens you can contact the Enagic® ECS Department to request the status on those accounts. You will be required to verify your account information, you can then find out the status of the open accounts and when they are expected to be paid off.

The last section of the report is the "Method" section. This indicates the payment method. There are basically only two types of methods listed, plain digits, which indicate that a full payment was made when the machine was purchased, or a star followed by a number and additional digits. The star indicates that the purchase was made using the Enagic® in-house financing plan and the number immediately following the star is how many months the purchase was financed.

These are the basic sections of the sales report. As long as you understand these pieces you should be able to follow and track the progress of your sales group and your Enagic® business. If you ever have any questions about the sales report or need additional help is best to contact your referrer first and then, if needed, contact Enagic® for further assistance.

NOTES:

PROTECT THE SHIP

This is the last topic in the distributor essentials section, and perhaps the most important. If you are serious about building a business as an Enagic® Distributor, you need to be SUPER serious about protecting the ship...which is Enagic®.

If you think about the Enagic® company as the vessel to your success, then you can understand why protecting this vessel is important. If the ship sinks, you go down with it! In order to protect the ship, you need to understand the things that could potentially sink it. The biggest threat we have to our vessel of success does not come from the competition, or the pharmaceutical industry or companies with an agenda that would make Enagic® their enemy. Our greatest threat comes from our own distributors.

Unfortunately, the thing that could sink this ship the fastest is medical claims being made by Enagic® Distributors. Because of rules and regulations set forth by the FDA, FTC and other federal and state agencies, medical claims that have not been evaluated can lead to BIG problems for the parent company.

While it can be very tempting for a distributor, especially a new one, to talk about how the water helped this or the water helped that, doing so can put the company in harm's way. You have to understand that making medical claims is VERY serious and that it is one of the easiest ways for this entire project to come to a screeching halt.

The Enagic® Policies and Procedures clearly states that distributors are not permitted to make medical claims; unfortunately, this only offers a small amount of

NOTES:

protection for the company. Because distributors are "Authorized" representatives of the company, ultimately the company would bear the consequences of distributors making medical claims.

And not only is this something that YOU should not do, but if you know of or hear of other distributors doing this, you should talk to them and explain how they are putting the entire project at risk by making medical claims. If they were to persist it would be your obligation to inform the Compliance Department of Enagic® so they could address the issue. Hopefully BEFORE it was to become an issue that could affect ALL of us!

Protecting the ship really boils down to distributors making decisions that do not put the project at risk. For the most part it is common sense. If you are not sure about something you are considering doing or saying, or if it seems questionable, err on the side of caution and DO NOT DO IT!!!

This business can be available to us for many, many years to come, but only if we, as distributors, commit to protecting it and making sure that we do not do or say anything to jeopardize the tremendous opportunity we have in front of us.

NOTES:

The Alkaline Water "Bandwagon"

In the last few years we've seen a number of alkaline water related products go from just a few to more than we can even count. While some distributors think this increase in alkaline related products is cause for concern the reality is, it is simply part of the natural progression of a successful product in the US marketplace. This is actually known as products jumping on the bandwagon.

Let's talk about the bandwagon effect, as it pertains to business, so you have a better understanding of what it is and what it means to you. Bandwagon is defined as: to join or give support to a party or movement that seems to be assured of success. Based on just this definition it is pretty easy to understand why other companies would try to introduce products that are almost assured of success.

Unfortunately, while a product is going through its lifecycle, this is when the worst of similar products will hit the market. It is still early enough that the masses do not yet fully understand the differences between a good and bad version of the product; yet people are becoming familiar with the concept and will buy a product if it sounds similar to what they have heard.

Typically the business related bandwagon effect describes how customers act, sometimes buying a product just because lots of other people are buying them. In this case the description is a little different. In this case we are actually taking about the bandwagon effect not inspiring consumers to buy, but entrepreneurs taking advantage of a developing consumer trend. During the next few years I expect to see a flood of alkaline / alkaline water related products

NOTES:

to hit the market. Why? Because consumers are learning the benefits of alkalinity and they are starting to spend money on these types of products. As soon as this happens, more and more other companies will jump of the bandwagon, singing the praises of being alkaline and trying to cash in on the trend.

It won't even matter if their product will actually help or will create any benefit for the buyer. They are simply trying to grab some market share, and make some fast, easy money, from the efforts of the people that have worked hard to develop the market to this point.

These other companies are competitors...kind of. There are two ways to define competitors. One is by strategic groups—competitors, who use similar marketing strategies, sell similar products or have similar skills. Under this definition, you might group other ionizer makers and Enagic® as competitors within the ionizer industry.

The second, less obvious way to group competitors, is by a shared customer—how strongly do the companies compete for the same customers' dollars? Using this method gives you a wider view of your competition and the challenges they could pose to your business.

These other products are not competitors, in that they offer a product that could compete with an ionizer, but they are competitors in that they are vying for some of the money consumers are willing to spend on an alkaline related product. Keep in mind that consumers are still learning the facts about alkaline water and alkalinity, so they will be easily convinced that EVERYTHING alkaline related is essentially the same.

NOTES:

Consumers do not know any better. The problem is that there are some companies that will not care if they dupe consumers; they will take whatever market share they can get, until consumers wise up and stop purchasing their product. Until that time, they will sell, sell, sell!

Don't be surprised if in the next few years you see not just a flood of alkaline related products, but a flood of ridiculous alkaline related products. As the term "alkaline" becomes more widely known, there will be hundreds of products that will try to maximize the trend. Some will simply add something alkaline to an existing product, like a food or beverage product; some will be all new, never heard of products, like alkaline chewing gum; and there might even be outlandish products, like alkaline shoe inserts or alkaline inhalers.

The possibilities are endless and, although we may never see these examples becoming actual products, there will be products that we would have never thought possible.

The reason that I am mentioning this is because I want you to be ready for it. I want you to be prepared for what WILL come as part of the success of this product in the marketplace.

It is not a matter of IF it happens; it is a matter of WHEN. Because it will happen. And when it does, DO NOT FREAK OUT! It is supposed to happen. It is part of the lifecycle and market introduction of a successful product.

While there is no need to freak out, there is a need to stay aware of what products are being introduced, what they actually do, and how to educate consumers about products that seem similar, but do not offer the same

NOTES:

benefit. In order to accomplish this you will need to become familiar with the alkaline / alkaline water industry. Watch television commercials, this will give you insight to the latest products and shifts in the alkaline trend. Do some online research every now and then.

Take a few minutes to search terms like "alkaline products" and then see what is happening. Stay up to date with new products and get familiar with what they say they offer. In some cases you may actually want to purchase the other product, just so you can see it for yourself.

Actually see, touching and taking apart some of the other ionizers on the market was one of the things that truly convinced me of the superiority of the Enagic® products. I got to see the cheap hoses that the other machines used; I saw the screw on wire connectors that were used only inches from water sources; I picked up models that simply felt like there was nothing to them.

All of these experiences helped solidify my belief in the Enagic® products. Don't be afraid of the other products that will enter the market. The reality is that most of them will not last. They will have their moment in the spotlight, but the light will dim as soon as consumers find that they do not live up to expectations.

As distributors we need to stay focused on our task, which is to share water and information. Don't get caught up in the craziness that will ensue as more and more alkaline related products hit the market. The choice is yours to stay focused on the task or get freaked out every time a new alkaline related product is introduced. You are with the best and no matter what other "similar" products come out, the fact that you are

NOTES:

with the best will not change. In fact, as some of these other products come, and then go, it may actually strengthen our position as the best. Because the best, in any industry, will survive and thrive, and we will, of course, continue to do both!

The Future of This Project

Many times when I am speaking with people the subject of the future of this project comes up and I am asked to share my opinion. Now please keep in mind that the following is MY opinion and is not necessarily the position of the company or any other distributor. It is purely speculation, based on what I know about market trends and other products I have seen in the past. I don't have a crystal ball, but I have experience.

As of the current state of the project, I believe that the Enagic® Independent Distributor opportunity has 10 – 25 solid years of growth and prosperity, maybe even longer. You may be wondering how I came to this conclusion, so allow me to explain.

First, you have to realize that the direct distributor portion of the project IS NOT going to last forever. It is not to say that Enagic® will not last forever, it is to say that the distributorship aspect of the program in its current form will not last forever; it can't. There will be a time when there is sufficient marketplace penetration to

NOTES:

make the need for independent distributors unnecessary or, at the very least, much less lucrative.

Once the product is main stream, meaning that average people from all over the U.S. and the world are familiar with the concept / benefits of alkaline water, the window of opportunity for distributors' closes and the door for the product to effectively be sold in more traditional retail venues opens. Now don't think that this is a bad thing, heck it is just part of the normal life cycle of a consumer product being introduced through this method of marketing. It is part of the natural progression of this technology making its way into tens of millions of homes across America and the world.

Having this happen and not knowing about it would be a bad thing. Knowing that this is going to eventuality happen keeps it from becoming bad, it allows us to take the appropriate actions and make strategic moves NOW!

Again, based solely on my opinion, here is what I think will happen over the next few years...

During the next 5 – 10 years, I believe that this product / project will explode from the Innovator stage to the Early Adopter stage, meaning that Enagic® will go from having sold a million machines around the globe over the past few decades, to selling millions of machines every year.

As you can probably imagine, this will create unprecedented growth for the company and will also create an incredible amount of wealth. It will also see the company experiencing "growing pains", which are the normal setbacks and hurdles that arise as a company goes from big to huge to massive in a short period of time. This growth will also create an incredible

NOTES:

amount of momentum in the area of product awareness, which will carry the notion of alkaline water throughout America like a flash flood.

I believe this is also going to be a time of increased awareness of maintaining a proper pH balance through the introduction of other pH related products. And I am not just talking about water ionizers. If you look around today you can already see it starting to happen. Television commercials are already introducing a variety of pH balanced products and touting their importance. Hair care products have been promoting the idea of pH for years, but now the pH concept is spreading far beyond the hair care industry.

In fact, I recently saw an ad on television for a new product called "RepHresh", which is a pH balanced gel used to improve "feminine freshness". Yeah, you read that right! You have to understand that what you see on television today is an indication of current or developing marketplace trends. Remember that the companies that are spending millions of dollars on television advertising have also spent millions on market research and product development.

There is nothing wrong with using the money that these other companies have spent as a guide to better understand the market. In fact, I often have a notepad and pen handy when watching television, in case I come across any interesting water related statistics, which has actually happened a number of times. And if you are paying attention to the television ads, you can also use the introduction of the other pH related products to further illustrate how the idea of pH is becoming more mainstream. Remember, if you have seen these ads, it is very likely that the people you are speaking to have also seen them!

NOTES:

Based on seeing more and more ads that focus on water and pH, I believe that during the next few years will see a lot of new products hitting the market. This is becoming a trend that is gaining momentum as more people are introduced to, and start truly understanding, the far reaching implications and benefits of proper pH balance!

I believe that these years of explosive growth will be the most lucrative for distributors. That during this time frame more Enagic® millionaires will be created than any other time in the history or future of the company. I also believe that these years will end up being the most important to every current Enagic® independent distributor.

I believe that the following 7 – 10 years will see the product entering the homes of about half the Early Majority, meaning that the number of ionizers in American homes will enter into the tens of millions.

Based on the current state of America and the world, I think that there will be a few major contributing factors that will greatly add to the success of this product and this project. You have to understand that there are other influences that can have a huge impact on the success, and in some cases failure, of a project. I think that during the next decade there will be a major paradigm shift in two aspects of American life: Health and Environment.

If you understand market trends and what drives them, it is easy to see why these two specific areas are preparing for major changes. Health in this country is poised for a major change due to two main contributing factors, the aging Baby Boomers and a greater

NOTES:

understanding to the how's and why's of the human body.

The first is the Baby Boomers. As I mention numerous times in this book, the Baby Boomers have been the driving force of the consumer market for the past 50+ years, and now is no exception. The difference today, however, is that the Boomers are moving from what they want, to what they need! In the past, what they have wanted has shaped the marketplace and dictated the products that were being introduced. Now, I believe that the same power of their influence will drive the market, but it will be based on the need for good health, a need that, without, will lead to the only other alternatives: horrible quality of life or death. Those are both pretty good motivators!

Here's where I think the paradigm shift will occur. You see, for the past 10-15 years, the Boomers have been forced fed the notion that as they enter their "Golden" years, the advances of "modern medicine" and "pharmaceutical technology" will allow them to pop a pill and counter act a lifetime of hazardous and irresponsible lifestyle choices.

Unfortunately for the Boomers, this pill is hard to come by and even harder to swallow! It's because the pill does not exist! In fact, they are finding that instead of finding a pill that will allow them to enjoy good health and quality of life, they are taking pills to reduce the negative effects of other pills. Instead of health and vitality, they are facing the greatest challenges of their lives. Their "Golden" years are being turned to "Tin" and they are rusting quickly!!

I believe that this will become a major contributing factor for a dramatic change in the pursuit of health and

NOTES:

wellness by the Boomers. I think that, based on their demand for something more effective, the Boomers will force the industry to make huge adjustments. It will also open the doors for many natural and holistic approaches to health and wellness to become accepted by the masses. This includes a newfound appreciation and understanding of the role water, specifically alkaline water, plays in overall health.

I think a greater understanding of the how's and why's of the human body is also going to influence changes that I believe are on the way. Every day we learn more about how our bodies function and what it takes to keep us in good health. I believe that the days of popping a pill for a quick fix are numbered and that the new found understanding of how our system actually works will greatly contribute to major changes.

Then there is the ever growing importance of environmental impact of everything we do. I believe that during the next decade, as the realities of just how much damage we have caused to the environment becomes painfully obvious to us, we will be forced to deal more directly with the issue of environment. This may come in the form of greater social pressure to be responsible or actual legislation. In either event, being environmentally sound will become much more important. Since our company and products already support an environmentally responsible way of life, we will be at the forefront of this developing trend. While others are scrambling to catch up, we will be leading the charge!!

I believe that these two factors, the paradigm shift of the Baby Boomers and the increased focus on eco-responsibility, will be the driving forces in the explosive growth that I see Enagic® experiencing.

NOTES:

You may be wondering, "What exactly does all this mean to me?" It means that you still have plenty of time to fully enjoy what this project has to offer. But it also means that you need to maximize every moment you have to build your business and take advantage of what we have today. You need to use every day to move your business forward. It means that you need to let other business minded people know that RIGHT NOW is the time to get moving with Enagic®.

NOTES:

So What's Next???

The next thing you should do is read this book again!! No seriously, you should!! Now that you have a better understanding of the project a lot of the information in this book will make a lot more sense the second or even third time around! You will be able to absorb information more effectively and the subtle lessons planted throughout the book will become crystal clear.

There are some other things you can be doing to help ensure your success. The first is to apply some of what you have learned. See how effective some of the techniques are for you. Try anchoring with a new prospect that you just started sampling the water and see if it works.

Commit to your own success and formulate your own D.M.O. (daily method of operation). Get yourself a calendar and make your schedule for this month and next. Go get some marketing materials and make sure that your team members have some as well. Make a brand new list of potential prospects and start contacting them. Get yourself and a few guests to the next presentation / demo or make arrangements to take them to the next available executive luncheon. Go get some bottles and sample a few more people. Start taking the steps to build your business and build it right!

The future looks bright ahead and you will achieve success if you take action.

NOTES:
_____

_____

SUCCESS IS WITHIN YOUR REACH!

YOU CAN MAKE IT HAPPEN!!

FOCUS YOUR POWER & RIDE THE WAVE!!!

NOTES:

Printed in Great Britain
by Amazon